At Issue

Are Unions Still Relevant?

Other Books in the At Issue Series:

At Issue

Are Unions Still Relevant?

Noah Berlatsky, Book Editor

GREENHAVEN PRESS
A part of Gale, Cengage Learning

GALE
CENGAGE Learning·

Detroit • New York • San Francisco • New Haven, Conn • Waterville, Maine • London

Elizabeth Des Chenes, *Director, Publishing Solutions*

For more information, contact:
Greenhaven Press
27500 Drake Rd.
Farmington Hills, MI 48331-3535
Or you can visit our Internet site at gale.cengage.com

For product information and technology assistance, contact us at

Gale Customer Support, 1-800-877-4253
For permission to use material from this text or product, submit all requests online at
www.cengage.com/permissions

Further permissions questions can be emailed to permissionrequest@cengage.com

Articles in Greenhaven Press anthologies are often edited for length to meet page requirements. In addition, original titles of these works are changed to clearly present the main thesis and to explicitly indicate the author's opinion. Every effort is made to ensure that Greenhaven Press accurately reflects the original intent of the authors. Every effort has been made to trace the owners of copyrighted material.

Cover image © Images.com/Corbis.

LIBRARY OF CONGRESS CATALOGING-IN-PUBLICATION DATA

Are unions still relevant? / Noah Berlatsky, book editor.
  p. cm. -- (At issue)
  Includes bibliographical references and index.
  ISBN 978-0-7377-6151-1 (hbk.) -- ISBN 978-0-7377-6152-8 (pbk.)
  1. Labor unions. I. Berlatsky, Noah.
  HD6483.A684 2013
  331.88--dc23
                                                          2012033957

Printed in the United States of America
  1 2 3 4 5   17 16 15 14 13

Contents

Introduction

In 2012, Wisconsin voters held an election to recall, or re-place, Governor Scott Walker. Walker, a Republican, was elected in 2010. He then moved to cut the benefits of public sector workers and to end the union's ability to bargain collectively. Wisconsin law allows voters to petition for a recall, and the unions and the Democratic party organized a massive and successful petition drive to unseat Walker. However, in the election, Walker was victorious and retained his seat, defeating Democrat Tom Barrett, the current mayor of Milwaukee.

Walker's reelection was seen as a serious defeat for unions, particularly public sector unions. Many commenters argued that it signaled the beginning of the end of union power as a political force. For example, Governor Mitch Daniels of Indiana, who has also moved to restrict public sector unions, spoke approvingly of the results in a June 10, 2012, interview with *Fox News*. Daniels said that the vote showed that "voters are seeing the fundamental unfairness of government becoming its own special interest"—which is what results, he argued, when public workers have their own unions. Similarly, Charles Krauthammer, writing in the June 7, 2012, issue of *The Washington Post*, predicted that the recall election "will be remembered as the beginning of the long decline of the public-sector union." He added that the unions had used their collective bargaining power to take control of government policy, sidelining the electorate and bankrupting local governments.

Other commenters argued that the unions had been damaged but not destroyed. Aaron Blake, writing in the June 11, 2012, *Washington Post*, said that public sector unions are definitely weakening. As evidence, he pointed to polls showing support for unions dropping from 72 percent approval in 1936 to about 60 percent in 2007. Blake also noted that union membership is dropping. Still, Blake argued, "The fact that unions still have the support of at least half the American people is hardly insignificant," and suggested that unions will survive in some form.

T.S. Weidler, an opponent of public sector unions, reached a similar conclusion for somewhat different reasons in the June 13, 2012, issue of *American Thinker*. Weidler maintained that the law supports labor unions by granting them tax exempt status, rather than taxing them at the rate of corporations. He argued that unions will always have huge amounts of money and will always be a major political force, as long as the tax laws protect them. "[L]abor unions have more money than Wisconsin has," he stated. "They are not afraid of Scott Walker. They will not wither up and die anytime soon."

On the other hand, Greg Sargent writing in the June 5, 2012, *Washington Post*, contended that the law has seriously *weakened* unions rather than strengthening them. In particular, Sargent singled out the Citizens United Supreme Court decision of 2010, in which the Supreme Court struck down many campaign finance laws that put limitations on corporations and other large donors. As a result of that decision, Sargent said, corporations and individual wealthy donors, many of them from outside Wisconsin, outspent unions by eight to one. Sargent quotes Michelle Ringuette, an official with the American Federation of Teachers, who said, "It's pretty clear that the voices of ordinary citizens are at permanent risk of being drowned out by uninhibited corporate spending."

Despite the defeat, some commentators remained hopeful about the future of unions. In an interview with National Public Radio's Robert Siegel on June 6, 2012, Thea Lee, deputy chief of staff of the AFL-CIO, said that while the Wisconsin result was "disappointing," it was "only the beginning of a long battle." She argued that the recall election and the outcry against Walker's policies would make Republican governors think twice before taking on public sector unions in the future. She also pointed to a simultaneous successful recall election for the Wisconsin Senate, which flipped the balance of power in the Senate from Republican to Democrat. "That's a huge victory for the working families," Lee argued, "and that means that Governor Walker's agenda is going to be slowed down pretty dramatically." She added, "if you look at Governor Walker, he spent $50 million to barely hold on to his job, and he lost control of the state Senate. So in that sense, it doesn't seem like a resounding victory for him."

The remainder of this book will look at other arguments concerning the relevance of unions, touching on issues such as globalization, public sector unions, teachers' unions, and right-to-work laws. Different authors will provide contrasting viewpoints about whether unions will, and whether they should, continue to be an important force in the United States.

1

Unions Are Still Important

Michael D. Yates

Michael D. Yates is an economist, labor educator, and associate editor of the socialist magazine Monthly Review. *He is also the author of* In and Out of the Working Class.

Unions are vital to protect the interests and improve the conditions of working people. Union employees have higher wages and better conditions than nonunion employees. Unfortunately, labor unions in the United States have weakened. Top-down labor reform movements have not increased unionization. Unions need to fight back against the ideology that unions are undemocratic and harm workers. Unions also need to oppose US imperial foreign policy, which wastes money needed to improve working conditions for Americans in order to oppress people overseas.

The first edition of *Why Unions Matter* was published in 1998. In it I argued that unions mattered because they were the one institution that had dramatically improved the lives of the majority of the people and had the potential to radically transform both the economic and political landscape, making both more democratic and egalitarian. I showed with clear and decisive data that union members enjoyed significant advantages over nonunion workers: higher wages, more and better benefits, better access to many kinds of leaves of absence, a democratic voice in their workplaces, and a better understanding of their political and legal rights. What is

Michael D. Yates, "Why Unions Still Matter," *Monthly Review*, vol. 60, no. 9, 2009. Copyright © 2009 by the Monthly Review Foundation. All rights reserved. Reproduced by permission.

more, unions benefitted nonunion workers through their political agitations and through what is called the "spillover" effect—nonunion employers will treat their employees better if only to avoid unionization.

Unions Matter More than Ever

This assessment of the impact of unions has not changed in the second edition. What was said ten years ago is true today. I have updated the numbers, but they still show that *unions matter*. Other things being equal (that is taking two groups of workers alike with respect to experience, education, region of country, industry, occupation, and marital status), union workers in 2007 earned $1.50 an hour more than nonunion workers, a wage premium of 14.1 percent. This wage premium was highest for black and Hispanic workers, meaning that unionization reduces racial wage inequality. The union premium was even greater for benefits: 28.2 percent for health insurance, 53.9 percent for pensions, 26.6 percent for vacations, and 14.3 percent for holidays. These union advantages have diminished over the past decade because union density (the share of employed wage workers in unions) has fallen. This decline has also compromised both the union impact on inequality and nonunion wages and benefits. There have been many reasons for the decline in union membership and density. . . . However, we can say here that falling density means a tremendous loss for the working class: lost wages and benefits for all workers, still less response by the government to the needs of workers, and a smaller counterweight to the forces that have given rise to greater inequality.

Maybe unions matter even more today than they did in 1998. Working men and women are more vulnerable to a host of problems than they were then:

- Because of the electronic revolution, the radical reorganization of the labor process, and the political deregulation of important product and financial markets, employers are more likely to move operations to lower-wage parts of the United States and to poorer countries. They are also more inclined to threaten to do so. Try to buy U.S.-made shoes, toys, jewelry, and a host of other consumer goods. If your automobile is made in the United States, chances are good that it was manufactured in union-free southern states.

- Employers are more likely to contract out to lower-wage states and nations both labor-intensive operations such as call centers and higher-wage labor like computer programming and medical service work. When we make inquiries about our computers, our credit card bills, our health insurance, the person on the other side of the phone will very likely be in a foreign country.

- Deregulated globalization, fueled in part by antilabor trade agreements, has displaced working people in poor countries like Mexico from their land and jobs. Large numbers have come to the United States, intensifying competition in some labor markets, allowing employers to divide and conquer their workforces, and giving an excuse for xenophobes like CNN's Lou Dobbs to foment anti-immigrant hysteria, which helps to keep domestic workers' from seeing clearly that it is their employers (and the employers' allies in government) that are their true enemies. As we shall see, the influx of immigrants offers the labor movement new and enthusiastic troops for rebirth and revitalization.

- Over the last ten years and especially during the administration of George W. Bush, our government has been increasingly under the thumb of corporate interests. The failure of organized labor to provide a counterweight to this has allowed a corporate-political alliance to sweep away most of the safety nets that protect us from the vagaries of the market and the inevitable occurrences of failing health, old age, and workplace injuries. Our health insurance system is in tatters, with nearly fifty million people without coverage and tens of millions more with inadequate and expensive coverage. These numbers grow each year. Few workers have the once common defined benefit pensions, in which they are guaranteed predictable monthly incomes when they retire. Instead, the declining fraction of workers who have pensions must accept defined contribution plans, in which they put up the money, sometimes with an employee match, and then must decide in what type of stock or bond fund to invest. How much money is available depends on the amount they were able to put into their funds, the size of the employer match, and the performance of the funds. The social security system, which is well-managed, financially sound, and capable of providing decent pensions for all, has been attacked by labor's enemies in a propaganda campaign aimed at privatization. Workplace safety has become a dead letter as has the enforcement of our labor laws. Those programs aimed at the poor, including those who lose their jobs, have been shredded, less generous in terms of both coverage and benefits. Workers were encouraged to consider their homes as security blankets, assets they could sell or borrow against to deal with emergencies or just to supplement incomes. But now the notion that a house is an asset that always rises in value is another big joke, one made at the expense of the working class. All in all, we can say with certainty that workers have lost ground economically, while those who hire them and invest in their companies, those who loan them money or hold their mortgages, have taken what workers have lost and lined their own pockets. Inequality of income and wealth have not been as great as they are now since the 1920s.

- While our government has eagerly helped employers beat down their workers, it has just as fervently wasted hundreds of billions of dollars waging war. In fact, the two phenomena are connected. War spending starves social programs and socially useful public investments. The war in Iraq may cost as much as three trillion dollars, money enough to implement a national health care system, expand social security, and begin to make the public investments needed to restore the health of our badly ravaged environment. Wars also are always harmful to the rights of workers. After the terrorist attacks of September 11, 2001, the federal government put in place measures to deny the rights of many federal workers to unionize and threatened to invoke anti-terrorism laws to stop strikes. A climate of war is a climate of fear and accusation. One right-wing pundit said on Fox Television that a national health care system would encourage terrorist physicians, willing to work for less, to come to the United States. Here it is interesting to note that in Iraq, where the United States was supposedly engineering a democratic society from scratch, unions and strikes are for all practical purposes illegal.

- Compounding worker insecurity has been the collapse of two financial bubbles, first the stock market crash that began in 2000 and the real estate debacle that commenced in 2007. The recovery from the first was one of the weakest on record, and working-class living standards never returned to where they were at the end of the last century. Some were able to maintain their incomes or make up for money shortfalls by borrowing, with credit cards and by taking out home equity loans. Both allowed consumer spending to grow faster than it would have otherwise. Now, however, the bursting of the housing bubble has left workers with a mountain of debt and no way out.

Workers Did Not Join Unions

It is difficult to imagine that this litany of working-class woes can be challenged and eradicated without strong unions and a vibrant labor movement. What has organized labor done to redress the many grievances of those who labor for a living? One would think that the events of the past ten years have sown fertile grounds for the development of a powerful labor movement.

Whether the President has been Democratic or Republican, labor has gotten the short end of the stick.

Perhaps no phrase captures what has happened in the labor movement of the United States more than the old saying that "the more things change, the more they stay the same." When the first edition came out, labor movement activists and scholars in the United States had high hopes for the "New Voice" movement, which in 1995 captured power in the AFL-CIO, the nation's labor federation. Led by John Sweeney, Richard Trumka, and Linda Chavez Thompson, New Voice promised a thoroughgoing transformation. Union membership would grow again; labor's political power would reassert itself; international solidarity would become the order of the day. There would once again be a labor movement.

Thirteen years after New Voice's inauguration, not much has changed. Workers are not joining unions. In 1995, union density was nearly 15 percent. In 2007, it was around 12 percent. There are fewer union members today than there were in 1995. The private sector has so hemorrhaged union members that union density there is now about 7.5 percent, below what it was before the Great Depression. A few unions, most notably the Service Employees International Union (SEIU), have grown, but, in the case of SEIU, there is considerable controversy over the manner in which the union has gained new members, with critics arguing that its growth has not strengthened the labor movement.

Unions Have Not Benefitted from the Political Process

Organized labor in the United States has never had the formidable political presence of workers' organizations in other parts of the world. However, there have been times when labor wielded some political clout. The record of New Voice here is not a good one. The AFL-CIO and its member unions have spent hundreds of millions of dollars trying to get sympathetic politicians elected to office, and with some success. Yet this has not translated into legislation that empowers working men and women. Except for a couple of badly needed increases in the minimum wage, the opposite has occurred. Whether the president has been Democrat or Republican, labor has gotten the short end of the stick: "free trade" agreements, an end to most federal aid to the poor, worsening health care, more working-class people in prison, the refusal to enforce the nation's labor laws, and endless wars that have drained public coffers of funds that might have been used to enhance the lives of ordinary folks. And as critic of the labor movement Kim Moody points out, there is a direct correspondence between the increase in the amounts of money and effort labor has expended politically and the decline in organizing efforts.

During an election year, organizing is put on hold and tens of thousands of hours are devoted to getting a Democrat elected. If a Democrat is elected, nothing happens to make it easier for unions to organize new members, so unions are no better off than before. Once when I worked for the United

Farm Workers union, César Chávez ordered the entire staff to move to Los Angeles to campaign for Mayor Tom Bradley's reelection. Bradley didn't need us to win, and he had little power to improve the lot of farm workers. At the time, there were organizing drives and collective bargaining crucial to the union that needed attention. They didn't get it as we wasted our time canvassing for Bradley—a good example of what Moody is talking about. . . .

All things considered, it would be difficult to argue that New Voice has succeeded, even on its own terms. The new AFL-CIO was a breath of fresh air compared to the moribund and badly compromised administrations of Sweeney's predecessors Lane Kirkland and George Meany.

But the air has gotten pretty stale, so much so that new rumblings began inside the Federation as early as 2000. . . .

An important part of the employers' attacks on labor has been a relentless assault on the notion that collective organization and action are good things.

The Ideological Battle

[A] new organization appeared in June 2005—the Change to Win Coalition (CTW). . . .

CTW, now including the once iconic union the United Farm Workers, did break with the AFL-CIO, and in September 2005 in St. Louis the breakaway unions formed the Change to Win Federation. Just as they did with New Voice, many labor activists and progressives jumped aboard this new agent of change. Three years later, it is fair to ask why. CTW has made little headway in building a new labor movement, no more so than has the AFL-CIO. . . .

So first New Voice, then Change to Win. The more things change, the more they stay the same. Unfortunately, these two efforts to change the lives of workers have done little to affect what has really been changing, namely the conditions under which working men and women labor. In addition, neither New Voice nor Change to Win has done anything to change the ideological terrain. An important part of the employers' attacks on labor has been a relentless assault on the notion that collective organization and action are good things: Unions are outsiders interested only in dues money. The government is a denier of individual freedom and a thief that takes our hard-earned money. Its only legitimate function is to defend the country from the collective hordes bent on destroying our hallowed way of life. We are, each of us, on our own, and this is a good thing. When we act in groups, we inevitably act against our own interests and trample the liberty of others.

The labor movement has not challenged this world view effectively. It has not come out foursquare for publicly funded universal health care. It has not rejected *in toto* the imperialism evident in every aspect of U.S. foreign policy, one that endangers workers everywhere in the world. It has not begun a national discussion on race, the main divider of workers. Union organizers for Barack Obama have gone out of their way to avoid talking about race to members who have expressed reservations about the candidate. Labor has continued to embrace the reactionary idea of partnership with employers, which is a cornerstone of the program of Change to Win. Tellingly, it has, with a few exceptions, failed to educate its members in any but a superficial way, leaving them in the dark on the issues that matter most. In the internal structure of its unions, it has replicated its class enemy. Some union leaders sneer at the very thought of democracy.

We all need a compass to find our way. For workers, unions and a labor movement must provide that compass. They have not. Until they do, no amount of top-down reform, no new union federation, no increase in union density will provide for workers the freer and richer lives they deserve.

Bright Spots for Unions

Amidst the many failings and shortcomings of unions and the labor movement, there have been bright spots too. Not long after the first edition went to press, many unions joined the fight for global justice and against the uncontrolled globalization that had been driving wages and working conditions downward worldwide. The most famous struggle occurred in Seattle in 1999. But just as this movement was gaining traction, the events of September 11, 2001, created conditions in the United States that made it difficult for a labor movement so tied historically to U.S. foreign policy to continue to participate. To its credit, the AFL-CIO and many member unions did not give the full-throated support for the "War on Terror" that its predecessors had given to the war in Vietnam. And unionists opposed to it formed a group that continues to exist—United States Labor Against the War (USLAW). Fernando Gapasin and I described this group as follows:

> This organization, comprised of individuals, unions, and other progressive organizations is not only opposed to the U.S. war in Iraq but to U.S. foreign policy itself. Its statement of principles—a just foreign policy, an end to U.S. occupation of foreign countries, a redirecting of the nation's resources, bringing U.S. troops home now, protecting civil rights and the rights of workers and immigrants, and solidarity with workers and their organizations around the world—is remarkable in light of the sordid history of organized labor's support for U.S. imperialism.

Just as remarkable is that the AFL-CIO has not only tolerated USLAW but given it tacit support by itself condemning the war in Iraq.

Dan Clawson in his book *The Next Upsurge: Labor and the New Social Movements* describes and analyzes several important and successful organizing campaigns:

- unionization by women that focused on nontraditional issues such as child care;

- union alliances with community groups, most notably the famous Justice for Janitors campaigns of the SEIU, but also efforts by unions and community groups in Hartford, Connecticut to win affordable housing for workers;

- campaigns waged by Workers' Centers, sometimes independently and sometimes in alliance with labor unions. Janice Fine defines such centers as "community-based and community-led organizations that engage in a combination of service, advocacy, and organizing to provide support to low-wage workers. The vast majority of them have grown up to serve predominantly or exclusively immigrant populations. However, there are a few centers that serve a primarily African American population or bring immigrants together with African Americans"...;

- living wage and anti-sweatshop organizing, which have been successful in forcing many cities to pay workers employed by firms with public contracts a wage that would yield an income at least equal to the federal poverty level of income and compelled universities to stop selling apparel manufactured under appalling conditions in low-wage countries. College students have expanded their anti-sweatshop actions to include the organizing of poorly paid employees on their campuses.

Union Growth

Some of this organizing has born fruit in terms of union membership. During the end of 2007 and the first half of 2008, membership increased in two important cities—Boston and Los Angeles. In Boston, cab drivers, security guards, truck drivers, communications technicians, and home-care assistants, among others, added more than 6,000 workers to union rosters. Most of these employees were organized through atypical means, that is, outside the purview of the National Labor Relations Board. In Los Angeles, union density rose from 15.9 percent in 2007 to 17 percent by mid-2008, while in California it increased from 16.7 to 17 percent. Both increases reversed many years of declining density. Remarkably, union density also went up in the nation as a whole, from 12 to 12.6 percent. This is not enough time to establish a trend, but it is heartening nonetheless.

I am not as optimistic as Clawson that there will soon be a labor upsurge. Still, his book shows that there are important and interesting things happening in the world of organized labor. For the past twenty-eight years I have been a labor educator, teaching union workers and students in union halls, motel and hotel meeting rooms, in college and university classrooms, and through the Internet. I know from this experience that unions are as needed as ever, that there are thousands of thoughtful union brothers and sisters out there, struggling to rebuild their unions and give back to unions the local and national relevance they once had. There are union officers around the nation trying to mobilize and educate their members, not just to empower them in their own workplace, important as this is, but to help them grasp the economics and politics of the times in which we live. They are trying to build the multiethnic, multiracial unions and labor movement of men and women that will really mean it when saying, "An injury to one is an injury to all."

2

Unions Are Outdated and Harmful

Gary Becker

Gary Becker is professor of economics and sociology at the University of Chicago, as well as a professor at the Booth School of Business.

Unions such as the United Auto Workers (UAW) are declining in numbers and influence. This is because federal regulation has improved working conditions, so unions are no longer needed. In addition, globalization means that companies can simply go elsewhere rather than pay high union wages. The unions helped elect Democrat Barack Obama because of his pro-union legislative agenda. However, if passed, this agenda would hurt business and the American economy. Luckily, even with government intervention, unions will continue to become less relevant and less powerful.

Union members constitute a mere 7.5 percent of the private sector American labor force, only one third of its share 25 years ago. This is why the UAW [United Auto Workers, the major US car manufacturing union] is a dinosaur, a relic of times past when unions were much more important. The UAW's membership has declined by more than one third since 1970, and its membership is still declining at a fast clip. GM [General Motors, an auto company] had one quarter of a million UAW workers in 1994, but now has less than 75,000 workers who are members. It is rather easy to explain why in effect, the US has become a non-union private sector economy.

Union Decline

The rapid shift during the past several decades from manufacturing to services has been a significant contributor since the generally smaller service establishments have always been much less unionized than the larger manufacturing establishments, like steel mills and auto plants. Globalization has been crucially important in several dimensions. Increased competition from imports have undercut the higher prices charged by domestic competitors who are forced to pay large benefits to their unionized workers. In addition, if a union tries to raise worker benefits, and hence production costs, by a lot, companies often close these plants, and set up production in other countries where costs are lower. Government provision of unemployment benefits and rules about layoffs—including anti-discrimination legislation—and voluntary provision by non-union companies of health and retirement benefits, and codified rules about the treatment of employees in regards to hiring, layoffs, and discipline have greatly reduced the advantages of unions in providing such benefits. Border and southern states discovered that they could be attractive to companies if they had more hostile environments to unions than other states. When [Japanese car] companies like Toyota and Honda decided to set up auto factories in the US, they generally avoided states where unions were powerful, and instead mainly went to states where unions were not important. Now foreign companies produce more than one third of all cars made in the US. Much of the decline in UAW membership has been offset by the growth of non-union workers in plants owned by foreign companies. In addition, cars made abroad have been out-competing cars made domestically by GM, Ford, and Chrysler. As a result, cars made by foreign companies, whether in the US or elsewhere, now account for more than half the cars sold in this country.

Unions Harm the Economy

These powerful forces aligned against unions imply that the UAW and other large manufacturing unions are essentially finished, perhaps unless they receive major financial and regulatory support from the federal government. This is why the AFL-CIO and Change to Win went all out to get Senator [Barack] Obama elected president [in 2008]. Unions are said to have spent over $400 million during the presidential race, and had several hundred thousand volunteers make phone calls and house visits. They claim to have been pivotal in Obama's victories in closely contested states like Ohio and Pennsylvania. According to one poll, about 2/3 of the members of the AFL-CIO unions voted for Obama, and only 1/3 for [Republican candidate John] McCain. Unions strongly supported Obama not only because Democrats have traditionally been much more pro-union than Republicans, but also because Obama had been explicitly supportive of unions. He and Joe Biden as senators co-sponsored the so-called Employee Free Choice Act. This Act failed to muster enough votes in the present Congress, but unions have placed highest priority on its passing in the new Congress that has a much bigger Democratic majority. Such a bill would give workers the right to join a union as soon as a majority of those employed at an establishment signed cards saying they wanted a union. Under present rules, there must be an election by workers to determine whether they want a union, with votes of individual workers being secret rather than publicly expressed on cards. Any substantial shift of federal and state governments toward pro-union regulations would harm the American economy and the position of the typical employee. As [Economist Richard] Posner indicates, unions want greater monopoly power so that they can raise the wages and other benefits of union members above their competitive levels. Unfortunately, the effects of this are to reduce earnings for non-union workers, shift production outside the US, or toward states with less pro-union laws, and shift production in unionized plants away from labor and toward capital. None of these changes are beneficial to the efficiency and performance of the American economy, especially in a global environment. Although the union leadership believes the Employee Free Choice Act and related legislation could add several million members, the good news is that they are likely to be wrong. The forces I discussed earlier that contributed to the decline of unions in the US are very powerful, they will continue to operate, and they are extremely difficult to reverse. So while pro-union federal legislation might well slow down the decline of unions in the private sector of the economy, it is highly unlikely to greatly affect the downward trend.

3

The Great Recession Has Marginalized Unions

James Surowiecki

James Surowiecki is a staff writer at the New Yorker, *where he writes a column on business and finance called "The Financial Page."*

The Great Recession of 2007–2009 has exacerbated the unpopularity of unions. In the past, unions provided benefits to all workers, since the threat of strikes and increased wages helped even non-unionized workers. As unions have diminished in numbers, though, benefits to non-union employees have dropped. Now non-union workers are frustrated by their losses in the recession, and they see union perks as illegitimate. Unions are caught in a death-spiral, where less influence leads to less popularity leading to even less influence.

In the heart of the Great Depression, millions of American workers did something they'd never done before: they joined a union. Emboldened by the passage of the Wagner Act, which made collective bargaining easier, unions organized industries across the country, remaking the economy. Businesses, of course, saw this as grim news. But the general public applauded labor's new power, even in the face of union tactics that many Americans frowned on, like sit-down strikes. More than seventy per cent of those surveyed in a 1937 Gallup poll said they favored unions.

Union Support Is Plummeting

Seventy-five years later, in the wake of another economic crisis, things couldn't be more different. The bailouts of General Motors and Chrysler saved the jobs of tens of thousands of U.A.W. workers, but were enormously unpopular. In the recent midterm elections, voters in several states passed initiatives making it harder for unions to organize. Across the country, governors and mayors wrestling with budget shortfalls are blaming public-sector unions for the problems. And in polls public support for labor has fallen to historic lows.

The hostility to labor is most obvious in the attacks on public-sector workers as what Tim Pawlenty, Minnesota's former governor, calls "exploiters"—cosseted, overpaid bureaucrats whose gold-plated pension and health plans are busting state budgets. But there's also been a backlash against labor generally. In 2009, for the first time ever, support for unions in the Gallup poll dipped below fifty per cent. A 2010 Pew Research poll offered even worse numbers, with just forty-one per cent of respondents saying they had a favorable view of unions, the lowest level of support in the history of that poll.

The disappearance of unions from the private sector has radically diminished the threat effect, meaning that unions don't raise the wages of non-union workers.

In part, this is a simple function of the weak economy. The statistician Nate Silver has found a historical correlation between the unemployment rate and the popularity of unions. Furthermore, an analysis of polling data by David Madland and Karla Walter, of the Center for American Progress, shows that, when times are bad, the approval ratings of government, business, and labor tend to drop in sync; voters, it seems, blame all powerful institutions equally. And although organized labor is much less powerful than it once was, voters don't seem to see it that way: more than sixty per cent of respondents in the 2010 Pew poll said that unions had too much power.

Unions Seen as Just Another Interest Group

The recession has also magnified the gap between unionized and non-unionized workers. Union workers, on average, get paid more than their non-unionized counterparts—most estimates put the difference at around fifteen per cent—and that wage premium widens during recessions. Similarly, union workers often still have defined-benefit pensions, which sets them apart from all those Americans who watched their retirement accounts get ravaged by the financial crisis. That's given rise to what Olivia Mitchell, an economics professor at Wharton, calls "pension envy." This resentment is most evident in the backlash against public-sector workers (who now make up a majority of union members). A recent study by the economics professors Keith Bender and John Heywood found that, when you control for a host of variables, public employees are not actually paid more than their private-sector counterparts. But they do often enjoy good retirement schemes, and in states like Illinois and California politicians have agreed to hefty contracts with state employees and then underfunded the pension plans, leaving future taxpayers to pick up the bill. It's no wonder that people are annoyed.

Still, the advantages that union workers enjoy when it comes to pay and benefits are nothing new, while the resentment about these things is. There are a couple of reasons for this. In the past, a sizable percentage of American workers belonged to unions, or had family members who did. Then, too, even people who didn't belong to unions often reaped some benefit from them, because of what economists call the "threat effect": in heavily unionized industries, non-union employers had to pay their workers better in order to fend off unionization. Finally, benefits that union members won for themselves—like the eight-hour day, or weekends off—often ended up percolating down to other workers. These days, none of those things are true. Organized labor has been on the wane for decades, to the point where just seven per cent of private-sector workers belong to a union. The benefits that union members still get—like defined-contribution pensions or Cadillac health plans—are out of reach of most workers. And the disappearance of unions from the private sector has radically diminished the threat effect, meaning that unions don't raise the wages of non-union workers.

The result is that it's easier to dismiss unions as just another interest group, enjoying perks that most workers cannot get. Even though unions remain the loudest political voice for workers' interests, resentment has replaced solidarity, which helps explain why the bailout of General Motors was almost as unpopular as the bailouts of Wall Street banks. And, at a time when labor is already struggling to organize new workers, this is grim news. In a landmark 1984 study, the economists Richard Freeman and James Medoff showed that there was a strong connection between the public image of unions and how workers voted in union elections: the less popular unions were generally, the harder it was for them to organize. Labor, in other words, may be caught in a vicious cycle, becoming progressively less influential and more unpopular. The Great Depression invigorated the modern American labor movement. The Great Recession has crippled it.

4

Globalization Has Damaged the Union Movement

Jeffrey M. Hirsch

Jeffrey M. Hirsch is associate professor of law at the University of Tennessee, Knoxville.

The world economy has become increasingly international, and today it is easier for companies to relocate in other countries, or to outsource production to other countries. Labor unions cannot restrict the labor pool as they once did, since in the face of a strike a company may simply relocate overseas. As a result, unions have been considerably weakened. If they are to stay relevant, unions will need to develop new means of benefiting their workers that are tailored to the global economy. Any downloadable version is for personal use only. The source website may be accessed at: http://www.e-elgar.co.uk.

The world economy is truly an international one. Technological advances in transportation and communications have eliminated many of the geographic barriers to trade and systems of production. The more established economies of Europe and the United States are now routinely linked with emerging economies of regions such as Asia, Central and South America, and Africa. As European and Asian economies

Jeffrey M. Hirsch, "Employee Collective Action in a Global Economy," *Encyclopedia of Labor and Employment Law and Economics,* edited by Kenneth Dau-Schmidt, S. Harris, and O. Lobel, Elgar Publishing Company, 2008, pp. 606–607, 613–614. http://www.e-elgar.co.uk.

in particular have rapidly expanded in recent years, the market for a wide variety of products, and some services, has become increasingly global in scale.

Globalization of Labor

Accompanying this change in product markets has been the globalization of labor markets. Because companies can easily transport their products to buyers around the world, the geographic limitations on where those products are produced have decreased. Technology, particularly information technology, has furthered this trend. Increased informational capabilities allow employers to use a wide array of subcontractors, even in different countries. The increased use of subcontractors, however, raises new concerns for workers.

> *A major check on unions' ability to pressure employers for improved working conditions is the reality that employers are increasingly able to obtain labor from many different countries.*

A significant factor in a company's decision where to locate production facilities is labor costs. The result is that many workers throughout the world must compete not locally or nationally, but internationally. Indeed, the growing roles of highly populous countries like India and China in the global labor market are but the most significant examples of this increase in the global supply of labor.

This expansion of the labor market impacts employment levels, wages and other conditions of employment as employers have a growing number of options to satisfy their labor needs. For workers, this shift creates a need for new ways to protect and promote their interests. One means to further that goal is collective action, whether from traditional trade unions or newer, less traditional employee groups. Yet, just as globalization has affected the labor market, it has also affected the opportunities for employee collective activity. As companies' product markets have expanded globally, unions and other worker groups must engage those companies globally as well. However, the extent to which unions (the term 'union' will be used to refer to any employee collective action group) can accomplish this goal is uncertain. Much of this uncertainty results from the effect of globalization on the traditional models of union activity. . . .

More Globally Available Labor Weakens Unions

A major check on unions' ability to pressure employers for improved working conditions is the reality that employers are increasingly able to obtain labor from many different countries. Employers' demand for more expensive union labor will continue to decline over time as cheaper nonunion alternatives become more prevalent. The outsourcing of union jobs to a country with lower wages is a well-publicized example of this reality and represents a major fear of union and non union workers in economies with relatively higher wage rates.

The growth in the global economy has caused numerous problems for unions trying to limit employers' access to non-union labor. As a growing number of countries produce an expanding pool of workers who can perform work being done elsewhere, the demand for labor in any given country becomes more elastic [that is, as labor costs go up, the demand for the labor goes down more sharply—because cheaper labor can be obtained elsewhere]. Unions' difficulty in limiting the supply of labor is also exacerbated by advances in technology which have made outsourcing more cost effective and enabled companies to operate with fewer workers. Moreover, global competition often demands that employers have increased flexibility, a need that conflicts with the more rigid and slow model of collective bargaining.

Because of these global changes, unions are less likely to possess significant power over a given labor market. Consider, for example, a union's ability to use a strike to obtain benefits from an employer. Employers' resistance to a strike depends on numerous factors, including the number of supervisors or other qualified nonstriking employees willing to perform the struck work. In the short term, these factors are limited by geography. However, in the long run, an employer can take advantage of an expanding pool of nonunion workers worldwide to help mute the threat of strikes or other union pressure.

Even where the relevant labor market has a small supply of nonunion labor, unions must be mindful of the long-term consequences of strikes and other attempts to pressure employers. If employers have the option of moving operations or having some of the work done in a different geographic area, then the long-run alternatives to union labor expand and unions' power decreases. Globalization magnifies this problem. As employers become increasingly able to outsource work to other countries and more countries have more available workers with appropriate skills, unions' difficulty in limiting alternatives to union labor becomes more severe. Moreover, although government regulations can limit this competition and provide unions with more control over the labor market, such regulations become less effective in a global economy where many countries lack such legal protections. The result is that unions must seek alternative means to obtain improved work conditions for workers.

5

Globalization, Union-Style

Louis Uchitelle

*Louis Uchitelle is a journalist and author who writes about busi-
ness and economics for* The New York Times.

*Globalization has been a boon to American workers in some
ways. As international companies have established branches in
the United States, those branches have in some cases been more
friendly to unions than American companies. This is particularly
the case for European companies, where unions have been tradi-
tionally much stronger than in America. In some cases, European companies, under pressure from their own unions, have
promised not to campaign against the establishment of unions in
American branches. This policy of neutrality has greatly aided
organization efforts in the Unites States.*

T*he challenge is to raise U.S. workers' rights to the level that
European workers enjoy—not to lower their rights to our
level.*

Seated on a folding chair in a cramped union office in
New York, Wilhelm Ado, a visiting German labor leader, explained through an interpreter that he had come to help
American workers do what they can no longer do easily on
their own—organize themselves into effective unions.

That means establishing unions with collective-bargaining
rights and contracts that, once negotiated, are binding on
managers. American law gives workers the right to choose to
be represented by unions, but today that happens less and less

as managers, ignoring the law, block the process. With employers firing or harassing employees who try to organize unions, only one in seven organizing drives eventually produces a contract. So the American labor movement has turned abroad for the organizing leverage it is losing at home.

Wilhelm, a compact, 60-year-old, is a foot soldier in that campaign. In late July, he visited the United States to help the Communication Workers of America (CWA) organize workers at T-Mobile USA, whose U.S. wireless network is owned by Deutsche Telekom, the German communications giant.

In this age of globalization, large foreign multinationals are acquiring subsidiaries in the United States. Going native, they are embracing anti-union tactics they avoid at home, where unions often have legal recognition, respect, and political influence. The CWA is trying to exploit this contradictory behavior by embarrassing Deutsche Telekom into being as tolerant of unions in the United States as it is in Germany, or at least staying neutral during CWA organizing drives.

As part of this strategy, in 2008 the CWA reached out to ver.di, its German counterpart. Wilhelm led the fourth visit of ver.di officials to the United States in support of the CWA's organizing efforts. A former telephone installer, he rose to be a director of ver.di and, as such, holds a seat on Deutsche Telekom's board of supervisors. That puts him in regular contact with Rene Obermann, the company's chief executive. Indeed, ver.di officials occupy several of the board's seats, as provided by Germany's co-determination law.

Beyond engaging Obermann, Wilhelm and his union colleagues lobby shareholders and convene press conferences, hoping that descriptions of a worker's lot at T-Mobile across the Atlantic will stir up public anger in Germany. In case that is not enough, ver.di, with 2.3 million members, can appeal for support to the German government, which owns 32 percent of Deutsche Telekom.

"We want to take back to Germany the personal accounts of workers here when they try to organize," Wilhelm says. "We are meeting with call-center workers and technicians, and they will tell us about their own personal conditions, and I will go back to Germany, and the next time I see Obermann, I can tell him, 'This is what the workers told me personally.' Because the company always says the workers are happy in the United States."

The CWA has been trying for years to organize T-Mobile's 26,000 technicians and call-center employees. It even endorsed Deutsche Telekom's 2001 acquisition of the company, then known as VoiceStream, in the belief that Deutsche Telekom's acceptance of unions, required by German law and custom, would carry over to the United States and that the CWA's organizing drives could then proceed without interference from company managers. The organizing drives have proceeded, but unsuccessfully. Larry Myers, senior vice president in the company's human-resources department, says that T-Mobile "provides an employee-friendly workplace where our people enjoy excellent working conditions, competitive pay and benefits, and direct, open, and frequent communication with managers." The CWA, in sharp contrast, accuses T-Mobile of anti-union tactics. "It seems like they are not very open to the idea of neutrality, to put it mildly," says Hae-Lin Choi, a CWA official who speaks German, acts as an interpreter, and helps direct the T-Mobile campaign.

The CWA has been trying for years to organize T-Mobile's 26,000 technicians and call-center employees.

Neutrality is clearly not in evidence at the T-Mobile call center in Springfield, Missouri, where 300 people, mostly women, earn $9 to $10 an hour for a 40-hour work week, with infrequent raises. When CWA organizers first distributed leaflets there two years ago, repeating the process for a day or two every month or so since then, the managers disputed the CWA's right to leaflet from the sidewalk near the one-story call-center building, claiming the sidewalk as company property.

Turnover tends to decrease as people gain a voice on the job.

That dispute was settled in favor of the union, according to Judy Graves, a regional CWA organizer, but there was another, more daunting obstacle—high turnover. The operators responded readily enough to union organizers. Many, Graves says, contacted the union through the telephone number or e-mail address printed on the leaflets or gave their phone number to those who approached them with leaflets. Discussions followed, off-site and during off-hours, and more than a few operators signed up for a representation election, Graves adds. But then many were gone, resigning voluntarily in most cases, often exhausted by the pace of having to handle one call after another, in several-minute bites. Indeed, turnover at many call centers across the country is more than 50 percent a year.

"A union would stabilize, turnover," says Graves, whose own spirits were lifted during a visit to Germany last May where she met ver.di officials and handed out leaflets at the annual Deutsche Telekom shareholders meeting. "Turnover tends to decrease as people gain a voice on the job and just-cause grievance standards."

As globalization spreads, allowing corporations to play off workers in different nations, it also promotes global unionism. In the process, a cross-border labor movement is beginning to add muscle to American unions. The United Steelworkers, the United Auto Workers, the Teamsters, the United Food and Commercial Workers, and the Service Employees International Union are all engaged in the novel tactic. SEIU is perhaps the most successful to date. Working in part through UNI Global Union, a relatively new Geneva-based federation of 900 unions in numerous countries, it is managing to organize thousands of American security guards whose employers were acquired by foreign multinationals.

A prime target is the Pinkerton company, which, fittingly enough, began as a supplier of strikebreakers in the 19th century. Today, Pinkerton's owner is Securitas AB, a giant security company headquartered in Stockholm, Sweden, a solidly pro-union nation. Securitas acquired Pinkerton in 1999, and in 2004, it signed an agreement with three unions—SEIU, the Swedish Transport Workers Union, and UNI—in which the company formally agreed not to interfere with SEIU's organizing efforts in the United States. Even with this commitment to neutrality, though, the going has been slow. Six years have passed, and Securitas employees in fewer than a dozen cities have been organized.

That is partly because the company's American managers have resisted, despite the formal agreement. "They push back, they argue that unionization will destroy profitability, they threaten to quit if SEIU signs up their employees, and that makes Swedish executives in Stockholm nervous," says Tom Woodruff, SEIU's executive vice president. "They don't want to have to send Swedes to run the American operation."

There is a cultural acceptance of anti-union behavior in the United States.

That's one dynamic; there's another. "Many foreign multi-national corporations cooperate with unions in their own countries but consider that they have a license in this country to prevent workers from unionizing," says Richard Bensinger, a former director of organizing for the AFL-CIO. They often argue that they are not in violation of American labor law, embodied in the National Labor Relations Act, and when they are found to be in violation, the penalties are mild compared with those in many other countries. "There is an arrogance in their attitude," Bensinger says.

And an irony. Wal-Mart, staunchly anti-union in America, has reached collective-bargaining agreements in several Chinese cities, signing contracts with state-sanctioned unions. IBM, resistant at home, accepts labor norms abroad. "When IBM opened a plant in Sweden in the 1980s, it did not want to be union," says Richard Freeman, a Harvard University labor economist. "Swedish employers said, 'This is the way we do it in our country.'"

The right to organize a union and bargain for a contract is enshrined in federal law, but the procedure is complicated. In most cases, a majority of the workers to be represented must sign cards requesting a representation election. The workers must then, by majority vote, authorize a union to represent them in bargaining a contract. The Obama administration has proposed simplifying this process but has not yet pressed reform in Congress. The procedure is still drawn out, giving managers time and opportunity to throw up obstacles: discharging employees who participate in organizing campaigns; harassing others by demoting them or reassigning them to overnight or early morning shifts; cutting benefits; keeping organizers away from plant sites; calling all workers at a particular site to a meeting at which unions are criticized just when union organizers are about to hold a meeting to convey the opposite message. Such actions rarely encounter public scorn, as they might in European and Asian countries where unions are woven into the social fabric. "There is a cultural acceptance of anti-union behavior in the United States," says Christy Hoffman, an SEIU official who recently joined the staff of UNI Global Union in Geneva.

In sum, we are no longer the pro-union nation we were in the immediate post-World War II decades, when roughly 40 percent of the workforce was unionized and union contracts influenced wages and working conditions for millions of non-union workers as well. Cesar Chavez, the United Farm Workers leader, mounted his nationwide grape boycott in the late 1960s on the strength of public sympathy for organized labor.

The deterioration in a single generation is considerable, particularly in the last decade. Only 12 percent of the nation's workers (and just 7 percent of private-sector workers) are represented by unions today, with a further decline likely as union organizing dries up. The National Labor Relations Board (NLRB) reports a "precipitous drop" since the late 1990s in the chief means of union expansion: workplace elections to certify bargaining units. Only 1,304 elections took place last year, down 60 percent in little more than a decade, with only 44,000 workers gaining representation in the elections won by unions. That number, too, has declined precipitously.

What stands out in this data is the role of the foreign company operating in America. One-third of the dwindling number of companies organized successfully in recent years were foreign-owned, according to a study by Kate Bronfenbrenner, director of labor education research at Cornell University's School of Industrial and Labor Relations. One of her colleagues, Richard Hurd, estimates that one-half of all workers organized into bargaining units in the United States in recent years benefited from neutrality agreements. Most of them involved foreign companies with operations in the United States, but in some cases, an American company acquiesced to neutrality in exchange for a union's support in dealing with the federal government, or with state governments, on a regulatory matter or other issue important to the company's managers.

"All this started in the 1990s, accelerated a decade ago, and has accounted for a majority of new bargaining units in the last five years," Hurd says. As a result, successful organizing today increasingly means that corporate managers have agreed in advance to remain neutral, often prodded by overseas owners and unions.

If autoworkers and T-Mobile employees have not yet benefited from the new cross-border pressures, thousands of American school-bus drivers have.

"The law simply does not make it possible at the moment for workers to organize if management wants to resist," says Thomas A. Kochan, a management and labor expert at the Massachusetts Institute of Technology's Sloan School of Management and co-author of the study that found that only one in seven organizing campaigns produces a collective-bargaining agreement when management actively opposes the effort. Illustrating the point, Bob King, the new president of the United Auto Workers, points to foreign-owned auto plants in the U.S. The UAW has asked BMW, Volkswagen, Mercedes Benz, Honda, Nissan, and Hyundai, all of whose workers are organized abroad, to recognize unions at their American plants, or at least not resist organizing campaigns. So far, they have refused, King says, adding that the NLRB election process is "broken" and should be abandoned. "In the early days, workers did not rely on the law," he says. "They did sit-down strikes and direct action."

He singled out Toyota in particular for criticism. "It has had plants here for 25 years," King says. "It is unionized in England, in Australia, almost everywhere else in the world, and here it isn't, because we as a society don't stand up for a worker's First Amendment rights: freedom of speech and association."

If autoworkers and T-Mobile employees have not yet benefited from the new cross-border pressures, thousands of American school-bus drivers have. Rather than bus children themselves, 30 percent of the nation's school districts contract out this service to private operators, according to the Teamsters. Starting in 1999, a British multinational, FirstGroup PLC, headquartered in Aberdeen, began to acquire school-bus companies in this country, vaulting into first place in the industry in 2007 with the acquisition of a company called Laidlaw, then the largest private operator of yellow school buses. (The drivers are FirstGroup employees; the buses they drive are almost always school-district property, and while 70 percent of the school districts still employ their own drivers, the outsourcing of this task to lower-wage drivers is growing.)

As FirstGroup expanded its American operations (it also owns Greyhound and Ryder Trucking), it came under pressure from unions in Britain and the United States, often coordinating their efforts, to cease interfering with attempts to organize FirstGroup's American workers. In 2007, FirstGroup finally agreed, asserting in a letter to shareholders that its American employees, like those in Britain, "should be free to choose whether or not to be represented by a trade union through a secret ballot conducted by the National Labor Relations Board."

To enforce this stated resolve, FirstGroup appointed a monitor, William B. Gould IV, a professor emeritus at Stanford University Law School and former chair of the NLRB during the Clinton administration. Under this new arrangement, the International Brotherhood of Teamsters expanded its representation of drivers employed by FirstGroup from 14,000 in 2007 to more than 25,000 less than two years later.

Gould credits FirstGroup's chief executive, Sir Moir Lockhead, for the change of heart. "I was approached by Sir Moir, who felt that his reputation was being sullied unfairly, and also that of his company," Gould says. Sir Moir asked Gould to act as monitor and to investigate any complaint filed by either a union or an individual employee. "I explained to him that [the] Taft-Hartley [Act] allows employers to aggressively campaign against unions," Gould says, "and he pledged not to do anything that would directly or indirectly disparage unions."

Gould says that in his role as monitor, he has processed 130 complaints of unfair labor practices, nearly all of them charging that the company violated its self-imposed neutrality. For each complaint, he has sent an investigator to follow up and has filed a report. "I think a major factor in the adoption of this program—indeed, the dominant factor—is the commitment of Sir Moir Lockhead," Gould says. (Lockhead is scheduled to retire on March 31.)

In the trenches, local Teamsters leaders are also upbeat, although perhaps not as upbeat as Gould. Teamsters Local 671, for example, represents more than 500 of the nearly 800 schoolbus drivers in the Hartford area of central Connecticut. The final 150 drivers to join the Teamsters came in a spurt after FirstGroup dismantled its roadblocks and embraced neutrality in 2007, according to Tony Lepore, the local's business agent. With neutrality, the margins of victory have been greater in each representation election, Lepore says, and the contracts negotiated with FirstGroup have been more generous, with the union winning additional paid holidays, attendance and longevity bonuses, paid bereavement leave, and a top wage of $19.10 an hour for a 25- to 35-hour week.

"We might have eventually achieved the same results without neutrality," Lepore says, "but it would have taken us twice as long to do it."

In the cases where we try to organize without global solidarity, it is much more difficult.

As if to document that point, the Teamsters are struggling to organize the school-bus drivers of another British company, the National Express Group PLC, which operates in the United States as Durham School Services and has an 11 percent share of the private market, second only to FirstGroup's 42 percent. Highly organized in Britain, National Express shuns unions here, although in a submission last year to the British Parliament's Joint Committee on Human Rights, the company said it "has adopted policies to ensure full compliance with labor laws throughout all of our operations, both in the United Kingdom and the United States and Canada."

The Teamsters represent 4,000 of the Durham drivers and are seeking to organize many more. "We are in a pitched battle," says Iain Gold, director of the Teamsters' Strategic Research and Campaign Department. "We are trying to document their behavior. We are trying to engage their shareholders. We had folks at their annual meeting this summer letting British shareholders know how their company is operating in the United States."

So it goes across the spectrum. ThyssenKrupp Steel, the German giant, is expanding a recently opened steel plant near Mobile, Alabama, and the United Steelworkers is seeking to organize not only the 700 existing workers but those to be added—doing so not through confrontation but through an alliance with IG Metall, the German metalworkers union. The goal is to pressure ThyssenKrupp into a neutrality agreement. "In the cases where we try to organize without global solidarity, it is much more difficult," says Patrick Young, an official in the United Steelworkers' strategic campaign department.

H&M, a big Swedish-based chain of clothing stores, is unionized at home and in other countries. The retailer, however, has resisted unionization in the United States, specifically the organizing efforts of the United Food and Commercial Workers (UFCW), despite a neutrality agreement that H&M signed with UNI Global Union. The UFCW was a partner to that pact, and largely as a result, it has organized 1,200 H&M workers in New York City, according to Patrick J. O'Neill, the union's executive vice president and director of organizing.

"We haven't achieved our final goal, but we have engaged the company on a number of levels," he says.

Foreign-owned banks in America are yet another target. So are food-store chains, manufacturers, and DHL Express, a German-owned package-delivery company. The list continues to grow as foreign multinationals establish or acquire American subsidiaries and the nation's unions respond, not through in-your-face organizing campaigns but through pressure to transfer to the United States a foreign owner's commitment to labor back home.

Hae-Lin Choi, the CWA official, is guardedly hopeful that will happen in the case of T-Mobile USA. She notes that Deutsche Telekom is bringing in a new CEO for T-Mobile—Philipp Humm, the first German to head the American subsidiary—and that maybe he'll be more neutral. Perhaps the pressure from ver.di's members in Germany is beginning to have its effect. "It is unclear," she says. "Humm could go either way."

6

Public Sector Unions Are Vital for US Democracy

Peter Rachleff

Peter Rachleff is a professor of history at Macalester College, in St. Paul, Minnesota.

Governor Scott Walker in Wisconsin has attempted to cripple public sector unions. Walker and other right-wingers portray public sector employees as lazy and greedy. In fact, public sector workers do the vital work of keeping America's democracy running. Because public sector jobs are much more unionized than private sector ones, public sector unions are vital for the union movement, which in turn is vital for the protection of working people. Demonstrations against Walker in Wisconsin show that working people can ban together for political change and justice.

With the Koch Brothers[1] footing the bill for his campaign, Scott Walker assumed the governorship of Wisconsin on January 7, 2011. Walker's first action as governor was obeisance to the corporate class that put him in office: he gave $140 million in tax breaks to businesses, including Wal-Mart, and then screamed "budget crisis!" This move allowed him to introduce his "budget repair bill," which would require state workers to pay $5,000 to $7,000 a year towards their health insurance benefits and pensions.

1. David H. and Charles G. Koch, of Koch Industries, have funded numerous conservative and libertarian advocacy groups.

Scott Walker vs. Workers

Uninformed, public-sector-bashing Walker supporters see this as an overdue come-down in public sector workers' unfair advantages. But the scope of Walker's bill is much broader than public sector wages, benefits and unions. It is a salvo in the broader Republican war against working people and all unions, proposing radical positions in the right's plan to create a permanent under-class of non-unionized workers: 1) reduce public employee collective bargaining strictly to wages; 2) prohibit all public employee strikes (the National Guard is on stand-by in Madison); 3) eliminate automatic deductions for union dues; 4) limit collective bargaining contracts to one year; and finally, 5) require union members to vote each year to "re-certify" bargaining units.

Walker has gotten a lot more than he refused to bargain for from the good people of Wisconsin.

Of course, the bill also proposes cuts in public education and public services. And right behind Walker's "budget repair bill" is an additional bill to make Wisconsin a "right-to-work" state [which prevents unions from compelling workers to pay union dues], which would severely limit the powers of private-sector unions. The one-two punch.

Giddy with the alignment of Republicans behind him in the House and Senate, Walker called a special session to demand immediate passage of his "budget repair bill." Simultaneously, he sent a letter to every state worker, warning that there would be no extensions of current contracts beyond March 13 [2011]—a decree which would eliminate collective bargaining. He declared all of this non-negotiable.

Walker has gotten a lot more than he refused to bargain for from the good people of Wisconsin. Resistance started with students at the University of Wisconsin, who asserted their right to affordable public education. On Valentine's Day, a thousand students marched to the Capitol and delivered cards reading: "Have a Heart. Don't Tear UW Apart!"

Private-sector and public-sector union activists met in a forum the next day, committed to standing together, and called for public protests. By mid-Valentine's Week, tens of thousands of teachers and other public employees called in sick and headed to the Capitol, joined by thousands of high school and university students. Even public employees who had been spared the changes of the proposed bill, such as fire fighters and police, joined the demonstrations.

Public-sector workers are not on the dole: they are the worker bees of this democracy.

The ranks of protesters swelled from 20,000 on Wednesday to 35,000 on Thursday and an estimated 50,000 on Friday. Signs expressed their anger—"Kill the Bill!"—and also reflected their awareness of international citizens' frustration with the "austerity" measures preached by the hoarding guardians of global capital: "I Went to Iraq and Came Back to Egypt," "Walk Like an Egyptian," "Let's Negotiate Like They Do in Egypt."

In a rare display of legislative backbone, 14 Democratic state legislators went AWOL and have been hiding out of reach of Wisconsin state police, denying the legislature the quorum it needs to conduct business. On the day Walker expected to be signing his bill, with 50,000 campers in the Capitol rotunda, the legislature announced its adjournment. Inspired surely by the hundreds of thousands of ordinary people standing up for regime change in Tunisia, Egypt, Libya, Bahrain and elsewhere, Wisconsinites had shut their government down.

Public Sector Workers Struggle for Their Rights

America needs to remember who public-sector workers are. Public-sector workers are not on the dole: they are the worker bees of this democracy, of the agencies which provide crucial services (roads, parks, schools, law enforcement, etc.).

In 1935, during the Great Depression, when the U.S. Congress passed the Wagner Act (also known as the National Labor Relations Act), which guaranteed workers the right to unionize, three categories of workers were kept outside the law's reach: farm workers, domestic workers and public employees at all levels of government. While millions of private-sector workers would organize for increased wages and benefits over the next two decades, positioning themselves to benefit from the economic growth of the 1940s, 1950s and 1960s, public-sector employees fell behind.

Public employees realized the value of organization, and their membership in unions increased tenfold between 1955 and 1975. At key points in this period, public-sector workers brought their lower-wage status to public attention, despite actually lacking the legal right to do so.

> By the late 1970s . . . , the "social contract" between employers, labor and the government was breaking.

In Memphis Tenn., in 1968, municipal sanitation workers earning poverty wages struck. They provoked a civil rights upheaval which brought the Rev. Martin Luther King, Jr., to Memphis—where he was assassinated. In 1970, tens of thousands of postal workers, some living on food stamps, struck in New York state. Their actions inspired other postal workers to strike across the country, which forced the government to reorganize the U.S. Postal Service and increase wages, recognize postal workers' unions, allow them to bargain contracts and institute grievance procedures and seniority systems for promotions.

Public-sector workers' pressure on big city and state governments for new labor laws, recognition and collective bargaining rights was increasingly successful. Federal employees—the outer, less-mobilized tier of public-sector workers—also gained new status and rights thanks to the activism of their state and municipal counterparts.

By the late 1970s, though, the "social contract" between employers, labor and the government was breaking. "Stagflation," fiscal crises and deindustrialization undercut first the manufacturing workers who made up the base of the labor movement in the private sector, and then ate at the gains of public-sector workers.

When Ronald Reagan fired more than 11,000 federally employed air traffic controllers in 1981 for striking without the right to do so, he sent a signal that times had changed for all workers. Soon, deregulation, privatization, globalization and contracting-out threatened the economic security of workers in both the private and public sectors.

This new political economy, called "neoliberalism" because of its credo of the supremacy of the market, replaced the demand-driven Keynesian approach [which saw a larger role for government in the economy] which had been foundational to the political economic policies from the New Deal onward. Employers increasingly turned their focus to cutting costs (energy, materials, taxes and overhead, and, especially, labor), while government, the public sector itself, became the target of media punditry and right-wing political hostility.

Private-sector workers faced permanent replacement if they dared to strike; strike activity declined. In reports on "large" (more than 1,000 participants) strikes, the U.S. Department of Labor noted a drop from 300–400 strikes per year in the early 1970s to 25–35 per year in the 1990s; the current figure is less than 10 per year. Private-sector employers increasingly have blocked union organizing efforts. The percentage of the U.S. unionized workforce shrank from over 30 percent in the 1950s to about 10 percent today.

The Stakes Are High

The public employees and their supporters defying Governor Walker by sitting in the Capitol rotunda in Madison are crucial to our understanding of the stakes for workers in this moment and for the future. Public workers' rate of unionization—36 percent—is much higher than their private sector counterparts'—about 7 percent. Public workers today make up more than half the ranks of organized labor.

Media and political advocates of neoliberalism have encouraged more and more of the general public to think of ourselves as the "employers" of public employees rather than the recipients of the services they provide. Public workers' compensation is derided as a drain on citizen's taxes. Public employee unions' bargaining strategies of deferring wages for improved benefits allows demagogues to paint these workers as the recipients of "Cadillac benefits."

As under- and unemployment grind so many in the general population down, with the attendant real fears of losing homes and dignity, the seemingly stable jobs in the public sector, with myths of inflated wages and benefits spun endlessly through the 24-hour news cycle, grate and gall.

Unions are "the anti-theft device for working people" as the saying goes—and bashing them has been central to the right-wing neoliberal agenda in the U.S. since Reagan and PATCO [the air traffic controllers' union]. In Madison, the grassroots campaign to "Kill the Bill" is showing the world the ready alliance of all working people (95 percent of us) with unions, community-based organizations, faith groups and students.

The Wisconsin conflict is being closely watched in Ohio, Indiana, Michigan and Indiana, where emboldened governors have introduced bills which would undercut public employees' rights as well as their wages and benefits. Social networking sites reveal that people all over the world are watching Madison. One report on Monday, February 21, notes that supporters in 12 countries and 38 states purchased more than 300 pizzas from Ian's on State Street, to be delivered to Madison demonstrators.

The throngs in Tahrir Square [in Cairo, Egypt] stayed and swelled until [Egyptian dictator] Mubarak left the country in 2011. . . . Egyptian people know they have just begun their pursuit of regime change and democratic process. In fact, it is the union movement in Egypt which now joins with the youth to propose the structure of long-term change. Yesterday, a Cairo demonstrator displayed his sign for all on Facebook and Twitter to see: "Cairo and Madison: One World. One Pain.". . .

The right-wing spin on Madison as hippies trashing the Capitol is refuted hourly by images of the volunteer crews of teachers gathering recyclables and the widely circulated Madison Police Department's "thank you" to the citizens for decorum in pursuit of their right to protest. These new alliances made in the streets and rotundas are unions—spontaneous versions of the structured unions which gather workers' concerns and advocate for them so workers can do their jobs safely and sustainably.

From Madison to Cairo and beyond, as dis-organization organizes, working people are feeling their common cause and asserting their majority rights to life, liberty and the pursuit of happiness.

7

Public Sector Unions Hurt the Public

Daniel DiSalvo

Daniel DiSalvo is assistant professor of political science at the City College of New York.

Public sector unions have many advantages over private sector unions. Public sector unions can organize politically to choose politicians, thus effectively electing their own employers. Through contract negotiations, public sector unions also have immediate access to politicians, something denied to most interest groups. Public sector unions thus have great leverage to advocate for salary and benefits. They can also push for larger government and more jobs for their members. As a result, public sector unions contribute to government bloat and to outsize compensation packages. As a result, they have created government inefficiency and bankrupted many local governments.

When it comes to advancing their interests, public-sector unions have significant advantages over traditional unions. For one thing, using the political process, they can exert far greater influence over their members' employers—that is, government—than private-sector unions can. Through their extensive political activity, these government-workers' unions help elect the very politicians who will act as "management" in their contract negotiations—in effect handpicking those who will sit across the bargaining table from them, in a

Daniel DiSalvo, "The Trouble with Public Sector Unions," *National Affairs*, vol. 5, Fall 2010. Copyright © 2010 by National Affairs. All rights reserved. Reproduced by permission.

way that workers in a private corporation (like, say, American Airlines or the Washington Post Company) cannot. Such power led Victor Gotbaum, the leader of District Council 37 of the AFSCME [American Federation of State, County, and Municipal Employees] in New York City, to brag in 1975: "We have the ability, in a sense, to elect our own boss."

The Public-Sector Difference

Since public-sector unions began to develop in earnest, their importance in political campaigns has grown by leaps and bounds. Starting from almost nothing in the 1960s, government-workers' unions now far exceed private-sector unions in political contributions. According to the Center for Responsive Politics, from 1989 to 2004, the AFSCME was the biggest spender in America, giving nearly $40 million to candidates in federal elections (98.5% of it to Democrats). It is important to stress that this was spending on *federal* elections; the union represents mostly *state and local* workers. But given the magnitude of federal contributions to state budgets, the AFSCME is heavily involved in electioneering to shape Washington's spending in ways that protect public workers and the supply of government services. And so over that 15-year period, the AFSCME was willing and able to outspend any other organization in the country.

The political influence of public-sector unions is probably greatest, however, in low-turnout elections to school boards and state and local offices, and in votes to decide ballot initiatives and referenda. For example, two of the top five biggest spenders in Wisconsin's 2003 and 2004 state elections were the Wisconsin Education Association Council and the AFSCME-affiliated Wisconsin PEOPLE Conference. Only the state Republican Party and two other political action committees—those belonging to the National Association of Realtors and SBC/Ameritech—spent more. The same is true in state after state, as unions work to exert control over the very governments that employ their members.

This political dimension of public-sector unionism also changes the substantive priorities and demands of the unions themselves. Although private-sector unions in the United States have engaged in leftist "social activism," they have mostly concentrated their efforts on securing the best wages, benefits, pensions, and working conditions for their members: "pure and simple unionism," as longtime American Federation of Labor president Samuel Gompers used to call it. Rarely do they demand more hiring, since—given the constant private-sector imperative to keep operating costs minimal—increasing the number of a company's employees can limit wage and benefit increases for the workers already on the company's payroll.

By contrast, as economist Richard Freeman has written, "public sector unions can be viewed as *using their political power to raise demand for public services*, as well as using their bargaining power to fight for higher wages." The millions spent by public-employee unions on ballot measures in states like California and Oregon, for instance, almost always support the options that would lead to higher taxes and more government spending. The California Teachers Association, for example, spent $57 million in 2005 to defeat referenda that would have reduced union power and checked government growth. And the political influence of such massive spending is of course only amplified by the get-out-the-vote efforts of the unions and their members. This power of government-workers' unions to increase (and then sustain) levels of employment through the political process helps explain why, for instance, the city of Buffalo, New York, had the same number of public workers in 2006 as it did in 1950—despite having lost half of its population (and thus a significant amount of the demand for public services).

For a case study in how public-sector unions manipulate both supply and demand, consider the example of the California Correctional Peace Officers Association. Throughout the 1980s and '90s, the CCPOA lobbied the state government to increase California's prison facilities—since more prisons would obviously mean more jobs for corrections officers. And between 1980 and 2000, the Golden State constructed 22 new prisons for adults (before 1980, California had only 12 such facilities). The CCPOA also pushed for the 1994 "three strikes" sentencing law, which imposed stiff penalties on repeat offenders. The prison population exploded—and, as intended, the new prisoners required more guards. The CCPOA has been no less successful in increasing members' compensation: In 2006, the average union member made $70,000 a year, and more than $100,000 with overtime. Corrections officers can also retire with 90% of their salaries as early as age 50. Today, an amazing 11% of the state budget—more than what is spent on higher education—goes to the penal system. Governor Arnold Schwarzenegger now proposes privatizing portions of the prison system to escape the unions' grip—though his proposal has so far met with predictable (union supported) political opposition.

Public-sector unions have automatic access to politicians through the collective-bargaining process, while other interest groups must fight for such entrée.

Freedom from Market Forces

A further important advantage that public-sector unions have over their private-sector counterparts is their relative freedom from market forces. In the private sector, the wage demands of union workers cannot exceed a certain threshold: If they do, they can render their employers uncompetitive, threatening workers' long-term job security. In the public sector, though, government is the monopoly provider of many services, eliminating any market pressures that might keep unions' demands in check. Moreover, unlike in the private sector, contract negotiations in the public sector are usually not highly adversarial; most government-agency mangers have little personal stake in such negotiations. Unlike executives accountable to shareholders and corporate boards, government managers generally get paid the same—and have the same likelihood of keeping their jobs—regardless of whether their operations are run efficiently. They therefore rarely play hardball with unions like business owners and managers do; there is little history of "union busting" in government.

Additionally, the rise and fall of businesses in the private sector means that unions must constantly engage in organizing efforts, reaching out to employees of newly created companies. In government agencies, on the other hand, once a union organizes workers, they usually remain organized—because the government doesn't go out of business. Public-employee unions can thus maintain membership levels with much less effort than can private-sector unions.

Finally, public-sector unions enjoy a privileged position in relation not only to their private-sector counterparts but also to other interest groups. Public-sector unions have automatic access to politicians through the collective-bargaining process, while other interest groups must fight for such entrée. Government unions can also more easily mobilize their members for electoral participation than other interest groups can—since they are able to apply pressure at the workplace and, in many cases, can even arrange for time off and other benefits to make members' political activism easier. Furthermore, most interest groups must devote a great deal of time and effort to fundraising; public-sector unions, on the other hand, enjoy a steady, reliable revenue stream, as union dues are deducted directly from members' paychecks (often by government, which drastically reduces the unions' administrative costs).

Taken together, the intrinsic advantages that public-sector unions enjoy over private-sector advocacy groups (including private-sector unions) have given organized government laborers enormous power over government at the local, state, and federal levels; to shape public finances and fiscal policy; and to influence the very spirit of our democracy. The results, unfortunately, have not always been pretty.

A Unionized Government

The effects of public-sector unionism can be grouped under three broad headings. The first centers on compensation, which includes wages, pensions, health care, and other benefits easily valued in monetary terms—the core issues at stake in collective-bargaining negotiations. The second involves the amount of government employment, or the size of government, as reflected in the number of workers and in public budgets. The third involves the productivity and efficiency of government services. Insofar as unions negotiate detailed work rules, they share the power to shape the day-to-day responsibilities of public servants—which influences what government does, and how well it does it.

These are complex matters that are hard for social scientists to measure, and on which scholars disagree. Nevertheless, the evidence supports a few broad conclusions.

In [2006] . . . , 225 of the 2,338 Massachusetts State Police officers made more than the $140,535 annual salary earned by the state's governor.

Most economists agree that public-sector unions' political power leads to more government spending. And recently, Chris Edwards of the Cato Institute [a libertarian think-tank] documented *how* government unionism has abetted growth in public-sector compensation. Generally speaking, the public sector pays more than the private sector for jobs at the low end of the labor market, while the private sector pays more for jobs at the high end. For janitors and secretaries, for instance, the public sector offers an appreciably better deal than the private economy: According to the Bureau of Labor Statistics, the average annual salary for the roughly 330,000 office clerks who work in government was almost $27,000 in 2005, while the 2.7 million in the private sector received an average pay of just under $23,000. Nationwide, among the 108,000 janitors who work in government, the average salary was $23,700; the average salary of the 2 million janitors working in the private sector, meanwhile, was $19,800.

For workers with advanced degrees, however, the public-sector pay scale is likely to be slightly below the private-sector benchmark. Private-sector economists, for instance, earn an average of $99,000 a year, compared to the $69,000 earned by their government colleagues. And accountants in the corporate world earn average annual salaries of $52,000, compared to $48,000 for their public-sector counterparts.

Not as easily captured is the comparable worth of those government workers who lack counterparts in the private sector, such as policemen, firefighters, and corrections officers. But that very monopoly status has given the union representatives of these workers enormous leverage, which they have converted into major gains. For example, in New York state, county police officers were paid an average salary of $121,000 a year in 2006. In that same year, according to the *Boston Globe*, 225 of the 2,338 Massachusetts State Police officers made more than the $140,535 annual salary earned by the state's governor. Four state troopers received more than $200,000, and 123 others were paid more than $150,000. While people whose jobs entail greater risk of life and limb certainly deserve higher pay, union power has clearly added a substantial premium.

When all jobs are considered, state and local public-sector workers today earn, on average, $14 more per hour in total compensation (wages and benefits) than their private-sector counterparts. The *New York Times* has reported that public-sector wages and benefits over the past decade have grown *twice* as fast as those in the private sector. These aggregate pay differentials stem partly from the fact that government work tends to be more white-collar, and that public employees tend to be better educated and more experienced, and to live in urban areas. Another factor is the hollowing out of the middle of the income distribution in the private sector. But union influence still plays a major role.

When unions have not been able to secure increases in wages and salaries, they have turned their attention to benefits. *USA Today* journalist Dennis Cauchon notes that, since 2002, for every $1-an-hour pay increase, public employees have gotten $1.17 in new benefits; private-sector workers, meanwhile, have received just 58 cents in added benefits. Of special interest to the unions has been health care: Across the nation, 86% of state- and local-government workers have access to employer-provided health insurance, while only 45% of private-sector workers do. In many cases, these plans involve meager contributions from employees, or none at all—in New Jersey, for instance, 88% of public-school teachers pay nothing toward their insurance premiums.

In Illinois . . . , public-sector unions have helped create a situation in which the state's pension funds report a liability of more than $100 billion, at least 50% of it unfunded.

Pensions Are Draining State Budgets

The unions' other cherished benefit is public-employee pensions. In California, for example, state workers often retire at 55 years of age with pensions that exceed what they were paid during most of their working years. In New York City, firefighters and police officers may retire after 20 years of service at half pay—which means that, at a time when life expectancy is nearly 80 years, New York City is paying benefits to 10,000 retired cops who are less than 50 years old. Those benefits quickly add up: In 2006, the annual pension benefit for a new retiree averaged just under $73,000 (and the full amount is exempt from state and local taxes).

How, one might ask, were policymakers ever convinced to agree to such generous terms? As it turns out, many lawmakers found that increasing pensions was very good politics. They placated unions with future pension commitments, and then turned around, borrowed the money appropriated for the pensions, and spent it paying for public services in the here and now. Politicians liked this scheme because they could satisfy the unions, provide generous public services without raising taxes to pay for them, and even sometimes get around balanced-budget requirements.

Unfortunately, the hit pension funds took recently in the stock market has exposed the massive underfunding that results from states' and municipalities' not paying for the public services they consume. In Illinois, for example, public-sector unions have helped create a situation in which the state's pension funds report a liability of more than $100 billion, at least 50% of it unfunded. Yet many analysts believe the figure is much higher; without a steep economic recovery, the Prairie State is looking at insolvency. Indeed, Northwestern University finance professor Joshua Rauh puts the date of collapse at 2018; he also predicts that six other states—Connecticut, Indiana, New Jersey, Hawaii, Louisiana, and Oklahoma—will see their pension funds dry up before the end of fiscal year 2020. What's more, according to the Pew Center on the States, 18 states face long-term pension liabilities in excess of $10 billion. In the case of California, like that of Illinois, the unfunded pension liability exceeds $50 billion. In fact, Pew estimates that, when retiree health-care costs are added to pension obligations, the unfunded liabilities of the states total an astounding $1 trillion.

The skyrocketing costs of public employees' pensions now present a huge challenge to state and local governments. If allowed to persist, such massive obligations will inevitably force a fundamental re-ordering of government priorities. After all, if government must spend more on pensions, it cannot spend more on schools, roads, and relief for the poor—in other words, the basic functions people expect their governments to perform. But because many states' pension commitments are constitutionally guaranteed, there is no easy way out of this financial sink hole. Recent court decisions indicate that pension obligations will have to be fulfilled even if governments declare bankruptcy—because while federal law allows bankruptcy judges to change pension and health-care packages in the private sector, it forbids such changes in public employees' agreements.

Government Efficiency Is Reduced

Yet as skilled as the unions may be in drawing on taxpayer dollars, many observers argue that their greater influence is felt in the quality of the government services taxpayers receive in return. In his book *The Warping of Government Work*, Harvard public-policy scholar John Donahue explains how public-employee unions have reduced government efficiency and responsiveness. With poor prospects in the ultra-competitive private sector, government work is increasingly desirable for those with limited skills; at the opposite end of the spectrum, the wage compression imposed by unions and civil-service rules makes government employment less attractive to those whose abilities are in high demand. Consequently, there is a "brain drain" at the top end of the government work force, as many of the country's most talented people opt for jobs in the private sector where they can be richly rewarded for their skills (and avoid the intricate work rules, and glacial advancement through big bureaucracies, that are part and parcel of government work).

Thus, as New York University professor Paul Light argues, government employment "caters more to the security-craver than the risk-taker." And because government employs more of the former and fewer of the latter, it is less flexible, less responsive, and less innovative. It is also more expensive: Northeastern University economist Barry Bluestone has shown that, between 2000 and 2008, the price of state and local public services has increased by 41% nationally, compared with 27% for private services.

Public-sector unions thus distort the labor market, weaken public finances, and diminish the responsiveness of government and the quality of public service.

Influence Over Government Policies

Finally, insofar as government collective-bargaining agreements touch on a wide range of economic decisions, public-sector unions have extraordinary influence over government policies. In the classic model of democratic accountability, citizens vote in competitive elections for candidates offering distinct policy agendas; once in office, the winners implement their programs through public agencies. But when public-employee unions bargain collectively with the government, elected officials partially cede control of public agencies to unelected labor leaders. Many policy choices are then settled in the course of negotiations between office holders and unions, rather than originating with the people's duly elected representatives. Over the long term, these negotiated work rules can drive public policy in directions that neither elected officials nor voters desire. And once enacted, these policies can prove very hard to reverse, even through elections: A new mayor or governor—no matter how hard-charging a reformer—will often find his hands tied by the iron-clad agreements unions managed to extract from his predecessors.

Stanford University political scientist Terry Moe has made exactly this argument with respect to the education sector. "Teachers unions have more influence on the public schools than any other group in American society," Moe argues. "Their massive memberships and awesome resources give them unrivaled power in the politics of education, allowing them to affect which policies are imposed on the schools by government—and to block reforms they don't like." One need only look at the debates over charter-school caps or merit-pay proposals to see Moe's point.

Collective Bargaining Has Had Negative Consequences

Public-sector unions thus distort the labor market, weaken public finances, and diminish the responsiveness of government and the quality of public services. Many of the concerns that initially led policymakers to oppose collective bargaining by government employees have, over the years, been vindicated.

As a result, it is difficult for defenders of public-sector unions today to make a convincing case that such unions benefit the public at large. Their argument has basically been reduced to three assertions. One is that most public employees live modest lives, and so criticizing efforts to improve their lot distracts attention from wealthy CEOs and Wall Street bankers who are the real culprits behind today's economic woes. Another is that the unions defend the dignity of public service, thereby preserving a middle class that would otherwise be plunged—through conservatives' efforts to privatize such work—into the vicious race to the bottom that now plagues the private sector. Finally, government-workers' unions help advance leftist politics by keeping the labor movement hobbling along.

To be sure, there is some merit to each of these arguments, though none is especially convincing. But even if these claims were completely true and obvious, they would not offer sufficient reason to put up with the other, manifestly negative consequences of public-sector unionism.

8

Unions and the Public Interest: Is Collective Bargaining for Teachers Good for Students?—Pro

Richard D. Kahlenberg

Richard D. Kahlenberg is senior fellow at The Century Foundation and author of Tough Liberal: Albert Shanker and the Battles over Schools, Unions, Race and Democracy.

The American public overwhelmingly supports the right of teachers to collective bargaining. Opponents of collective bargaining argue that unions give teachers too much influence over politicians, and that unions protect incompetent teachers. However, the truth is that unions allow teachers to advocate for children, who are cut out of the political process. Moreover, unions have no interest in protecting incompetent teachers, who make teachers' jobs more difficult. In the United States and worldwide, school systems without collective bargaining tend to have worse outcomes for students than those with collective bargaining. This suggests that schools, teachers, and children all benefit from strong teachers' unions.

*T*hree years after Barack Obama's election signaled a seeming resurgence for America's unions, the landscape looks very different. Republican governors in Wisconsin, Indiana, and Ohio *have limited the reach of collective bargaining for public employees. The moves, especially in Wisconsin, set off a national furor that has all but obscured the underlying debate as it relates to schooling: Should public-employee collective bargaining be reined in or expanded in education? Is the public interest served by public-sector collective bargaining? If so, how and in what ways? Arguing in this forum for more expansive collective bargaining for teachers is Richard D. Kahlenberg, senior fellow at The Century Foundation and author of* Tough Liberal: Albert Shanker and the Battles over Schools, Unions, Race and Democracy. *Responding [in the next viewpoint] that public-employee collective bargaining is destructive to schooling and needs to be reined in is Jay P. Greene, chair of the Department of Education Reform at the University of Arkansas and author of* Education Myths.

Wisconsin governor Scott Walker's campaign earlier this year to significantly curtail the scope of bargaining for the state's public employees, including teachers, set off a national debate over whether their long-established right to collectively bargain should be reined in, or even eliminated.

If you're a Republican who wants to win elections, going after teachers unions makes parochial sense. According to Terry Moe, the National Education Association (NEA) and the American Federation of Teachers (AFT) gave 95 percent of contributions to Democrats in federal elections between 1989 and 2010. "Collective bargaining is the bedrock of union well-being," Moe notes, so to constrain collective bargaining is to weaken union power. The partisan nature of Walker's campaign was revealed when he exempted two public-employee unions that supported him politically: those representing police and firefighters.

But polls suggest that Americans don't want to see teachers and other public employees stripped of collective bargaining rights. A *USA Today*/Gallup poll found that by a margin of 61 to 33 percent, Americans oppose ending collective bargaining for public employees. A *Wall Street Journal*/NBC poll discovered that while Americans want public employees to pay more for retirement benefits and health care, 77 percent said unionized state and municipal employees should have the same rights as union members who work in the private sector. Is the public wrong in supporting the rights of teachers and other public employees to collectively bargain? I don't think so.

The NEA has existed since 1857 and the AFT since 1916, but teachers didn't have real influence until they began bargaining collectively in the 1960s. Before that, as Albert Shanker, one of the founding fathers of modern teachers unions, noted, teachers engaged in "collective begging." Educators were very poorly compensated; in New York City, they were paid less than those washing cars for a living. Teachers were subject to the whims of often autocratic principals and could be fired for joining a union.

Collective bargaining is important, not only to advance individual interests but to give unions the power to serve as a countervailing force against big business and big government.

Some teachers objected to the idea of collective bargaining. They saw unions as organizations for blue-collar workers, not for college-educated professionals. But Shanker and others insisted that teachers needed collective bargaining in order to be compensated sufficiently and treated as professionals.

Democratic societies throughout the world recognize the basic right of employees to band together to pursue their interests and secure a decent standard of living. Article 23 of the 1948 Universal Declaration of Human Rights provides not only that workers should be shielded from discrimination, but also that "everyone has the right to form and to join trade unions for the protection of his interests."

Collective bargaining is important, not only to advance individual interests but to give unions the power to serve as a countervailing force against big business and big government. Citing the struggle of Polish workers against the Communist regime, Ronald Reagan declared in a Labor Day speech in 1980, "where free unions and collective bargaining are forbidden, freedom is lost."

The majority of Americans believe that citizens don't give up the basic right to collective bargaining just because they work for the government. In free societies across the globe, from Finland to Japan, public school teachers have the right to form unions and engage in collective bargaining.

In the United States, only seven states outlaw collective bargaining for teachers. Thirty-four states and the District of Columbia authorize collective bargaining for such employees, and another nine permit it. It is no accident that the seven states that prohibit collective bargaining for teachers are mostly in the Deep South, the region of the country historically most hostile to extending democratic citizenship to all Americans.

Terry Moe finds that collective bargaining for teachers has strong support among candidates for school boards. He writes, "the vast majority of school board candidates, 66 percent, have positive overall attitudes toward collective bargaining. Even among Republicans—indeed, even among Republicans who are not endorsed by the unions—the majority take a positive approach to this most crucial of union concerns."

Nonetheless, some (including Moe) would prefer that collective bargaining for teachers be severely curtailed, or even outlawed. Ironically, one argument advanced by critics is that collective bargaining is undemocratic. The other major argument is that teacher collective bargaining is bad for education. Both claims are without basis.

Those who argue that collective bargaining for teachers is stacked, even undemocratic, say that, unlike in the private sector, where management and labor go head-to-head with clearly distinct interests, in the case of teachers, powerful unions are actively involved in electing school board members, essentially helping to pick the management team. Moreover, when collective bargaining covers education policy areas, such as class size or discipline codes, the public is shut out of the negotiations, some assert. Along the way, they conclude, the interests of adults in the system are served but not the interests of children.

Teachers, as much as any other group in society, can serve as powerful advocates for those Americans who cannot vote: schoolchildren.

But these arguments fail to recognize that in a democracy, school boards are ultimately accountable to all voters, not just teachers, who often live and vote outside the district in which they teach, and in any event represent a small share of total voters. Union endorsements matter in school board elections, but so do the interests of general taxpayers and parents and everyone else who makes up the community. If school board members toe a teachers union line that is unpopular with voters, those officials can be thrown out in the next election.

Indeed, one could make a strong argument that any outsized influence that teachers unions exercise in school board elections provides a nice enhancement of democratic decisionmaking on education policy because teachers, as much as any other group in society, can serve as powerful advocates for those Americans who cannot vote: schoolchildren. The interests of teachers and their unions don't always coincide with those of students, but on the really big issues, such as overall investment in education, the convergence of interests is strong. Certainly, the interests of teachers in ensuring adequate educational investment are far stronger than they are for most voters, who don't have children in the school system and may be more concerned about holding down taxes than investing in the education of other people's kids.

American society consistently underinvests in children compared with other leading democratic societies. According to the Organisation for Economic Co-operation and Development (OECD), the child poverty rate in the United States is 21.6 percent, the fifth-highest among its 40 member nations. Only Turkey, Romania, Mexico, and Israel have higher child-poverty rates. Put differently, we're in the bottom one-eighth in preventing child poverty. By contrast, when the interests of children are connected with the interests of teachers, as they are on the question of public education spending, the U.S. ranks close to the top one-third. Among 39 OECD nations, the U.S. ranks 14th in spending on primary and secondary education as a percentage of gross domestic product.

Reform plans [that weed out bad teachers] put the lie to the notion that the average teacher has an interest in her union protecting incompetent colleagues.

Some critics argue that strong teachers unions make for inefficient spending and bad education policies in the instances when teacher and student interests diverge. For example, it is frequently claimed that teachers unions, through collective-bargaining agreements, protect incompetent members and prevent good teachers from being paid more.

This sometimes occurs, and when it does, it is troublesome. But a number of reform union leaders, going back to Al Shanker, have embraced "peer review" plans, which weed out bad teachers in Toledo, Ohio; Montgomery County, Maryland; and elsewhere. These reform plans put the lie to the notion that the average teacher has an interest in her union protecting incompetent colleagues. To the contrary, dead wood on the faculty makes every other teacher's job more difficult. Likewise, numerous local unions have adopted pay-for-performance plans, when the measurement of performance is valid and incentives are in place to encourage good teachers to share innovative teaching techniques rather than hoarding them.

Moreover, many of the things that teachers collectively bargain for are good for kids. The majority of students benefit when teachers can more easily discipline unruly students, for example. (Principals, by contrast, often want to take a softer line so the school's suspension rates don't look bad.) Higher compensation packages attract higher-quality teacher candidates and reduce disruptive teacher turnover.

Reforms that draw on teacher wisdom are more likely to be effectively implemented when the classroom door closes.

If collective bargaining were really a terrible practice for education, we should see stellar results where it does not occur: in the American South and in the charter school arena, for example. Why, then, aren't the seven states that forbid collective bargaining for teachers (Arizona, Georgia, Mississippi, North Carolina, South Carolina, Texas, and Virginia) at the top of the educational heap? Why do charter schools, 88 percent of which are nonunion, only outperform regular public schools 17 percent of the time, as a 2009 Stanford University study found? Why, instead, do we see states like Massachusetts, and countries like Finland, both with strong teachers unions, leading the pack?

Opponents of collective bargaining will immediately point out that poverty rates are high in the American South, and low in Finland, which is an entirely valid point. But doesn't that suggest that the national obsession with weakening teachers unions may be less important than finding ways to reduce childhood poverty?

Moreover, scholarly studies that seek to control for poverty find that collective bargaining is associated with somewhat stronger, not weaker, student outcomes. Sociologist Robert Carini's 2002 review of 17 studies found that "unionism leads to modestly higher standardized achievement test scores, and possibly enhanced prospects for graduation from high school." Even Terry Moe, an outspoken opponent of collective bargaining for teachers, suggests that research on the impact of collective bargaining on student outcomes "has generated mixed findings (so far) and doesn't provide definitive answers."

For a variety of reasons, collective bargaining for teachers should not be constrained, much less eliminated. Indeed, if teachers are to be partners in innovative education reform, the scope of collective bargaining should be expanded. When the United Federation of Teachers first began to bargain collectively in the early 1960s, Albert Shanker was distressed that the New York City school board was willing to discuss only traditional issues like wages and benefits and rejected the idea of bargaining over broader policies that the union proposed, such as the creation of magnet schools.

Shanker saw that by reducing the scope of collective bargaining, critics created a political trap for unions. Union leaders were told they could only address bread-and-butter issues and then were criticized for caring only about their own selfish concerns rather than student achievement or larger policy issues. Moreover, Shanker believed that teachers had a lot of good ideas that could be incorporated into collective bargaining agreements, such as teacher peer review, suggestions for the types of curricula that work best in the classroom, and what sorts of programs would lure teachers into high-poverty schools. He also knew that reforms that draw on teacher wisdom are more likely to be effectively implemented when the classroom door closes.

In the end, Shanker's frustration with the traditional constraints of collective bargaining spurred him to propose, in a

1988 speech at the National Press Club, the creation of "charter schools," where teachers would draw upon a wealth of experience to try innovative ideas. Much to Shanker's dismay, the charter school movement went in a very different direction, becoming a vehicle for avoiding unions and reducing teacher voice (and thereby increasing teacher turnover). And charters still educate a very small fraction of students.

Expanding collective bargaining for teachers to more states and to more education issues will give educators greater voice, and in so doing, indirectly strengthen the voice of students. Overall, the evidence suggests that Scott Walker has it exactly wrong, and the American public, which overwhelmingly supports the right to collective bargaining, has it right.

Jay Greene's opening line, comparing teachers unions to the Tobacco Institute, is very telling about his overall analysis. He's right, of course, that both are "interest groups," but does he not see a massive difference between an entity that is devoted to getting more kids addicted to deadly cigarettes so they'll be lifelong clients and a group representing rank-and-file teachers whose life's work is educating children?

Greene complains that teachers unions have become "more militant in recent years." But teacher strikes, which were quite common in the 1960s and 1970s, dropped 90 percent by the mid-1980s and are now, as one education report noted, essentially "relics of the past." To the extent that teachers have rallied, it's in response to unprecedented attacks on them in places like Wisconsin, where a half century of labor law was radically rewritten. Astonishingly, Greene would go further than Wisconsin Republicans and "return to the pre-collective bargaining era."

Greene says providing teachers with better pay and benefits is bad for kids, but where is his evidence? Don't better compensation packages attract brighter talent, or are the laws of supply and demand suddenly suspended when it comes to teachers?

Finally, Greene is correct to suggest that teacher and student interests are not perfectly aligned, but who are the selfless adults who better represent the interests of kids? The hedge fund managers who support charter schools and also want their income taxed at lower rates than regular earned income, thereby squeezing education budgets? Superintendents who sometimes junk promising initiatives for which they cannot take credit? I'd rather place my faith in the democratically elected representatives of educators who work with kids day in and day out.

9

Unions and the Public Interest: Is Collective Bargaining for Teachers Good for Students?—Con

Jay P. Greene

Jay P. Greene is chair of the Department of Education Reform at the University of Arkansas and author of Education Myths.

Teachers' unions are organized interest groups that promote the interests of their own members (teachers), even at the expense of the interests of nonmembers (students, parents, and other taxpayers). The normal checks and balances, however, to the promotion of a group's self-interest have failed in the area of education. The concentration of educators at schools and the geographic dispersion of parents and other taxpayers give an advantage to teachers in terms of the ability to organize. In addition, teachers' unions have been effective at getting people to believe that teachers are as interested in their children as the parents are, though the unions themselves are about acquiring power to advocate for their members. Finally, teachers can organize and vote for candidates that favor the union's interests, so that nonmember interests are not well represented during the bargaining process. A better way to improve compensation and working conditions for teachers is through changes in law and regulation, rather than through collective bargaining.

Asking if teachers unions are a positive force in education is a bit like asking if the Tobacco Institute is a positive force in health policy or if the sugar lobby is helpful in assessing the merits of corn syrup. The problem is not that teachers unions are hostile to the interests of students and their families, but that teachers unions, like any organized interest group, are specifically designed to promote the interests of their own members and not to safeguard the interests of nonmembers. To the extent that teachers benefit from more generous pay and benefits, less-demanding work conditions, and higher job security, the unions will pursue those goals, even if achieving them comes at the expense of students. That is what interest groups do. Unfortunately, a public education system that guarantees ever-increasing pay and benefits while lowering work demands on teachers, who virtually hold their positions for life regardless of performance, harms students.

Collective bargaining is the primary vehicle through which the unions enact their preferred policies regarding pay, benefits, job security, and work conditions. It is also the mechanism by which unions collect fees from teachers that provide them with the resources to prevail politically. Until the ability of teachers unions to engage in collective bargaining is restrained, we should expect unions to continue to use it to advance the interests of their adult members over those of children, their families, and taxpayers.

Teachers unions only won the privilege of engaging in collective bargaining in the last 50 years, about when student achievement began to stagnate and costs to soar. A return to the pre-collective bargaining era may be the tonic our education system needs to return to growth in achievement and restraint in costs.

The nature and function of organized interest groups is widely known and understood. Of course, there is nothing wrong with people organizing interest groups to advocate for themselves. That is an essential part of the freedom of assembly, protected by the U.S. Constitution. If people dislike what an interest group is advocating, they can organize other interest groups to compete in the marketplace of ideas and advocate for other concerns. The normal process of checks and balances among competing interest groups, however, has failed when it comes to education.

The problem is not that teachers unions are hostile to the interests of students and their families, but that teachers unions, like any organized interest group, are specifically designed to promote the interests of their own members and not to safeguard the interests of nonmembers.

There are three factors that have contributed to the failure of other groups to check the power of teachers unions. First, there is an asymmetry in the ability of groups to organize in education, significantly favoring the teachers unions. Teachers unions have a huge advantage in organizing and advocating for their interests. Employees of the public school system are physically concentrated in school buildings, making it easier for them to organize. And because current employees are in a good position to know how they can benefit from the system, they can be mobilized relatively easily to advocate for those policies. Parents, taxpayers, and members of the general public are geographically dispersed, making it harder for them to organize. And because they are not immersed in education matters, they cannot easily envision how policy changes might help or hurt, making it harder to mobilize them on those issues. It is hardly unique to education that concentrated interests have an advantage over diffuse interests, but this is one factor contributing to teachers union dominance.

Second, teachers unions have fooled a large section of the general public and elites into thinking of them as something other than a regular interest group advocating for their own concerns.

The teachers unions have worked hard to convince people that they are a collection of educators who love our children almost as much as the parents do. They're like the favorite aunt or uncle who dotes on our children. This image of the teachers unions as part of our family is facilitated by the fact that virtually every college-educated household (the households with the greatest political influence) has at least one current or former public school teacher sitting at the dining table when they gather for Thanksgiving. This impression is also fostered by ad campaigns featuring teachers buying school supplies out of their own pockets and movie portraits of heroic teachers believing in students, even as their parents have abandoned them.

Of course, some teachers really do buy school supplies with their own money (which should make people wonder what kind of education system would make that necessary after spending an average of more than $12,000 per student each year). And some teachers really are like the doting aunt or uncle who sticks with kids, even when the parents have given up. But loving children and being part of the family is certainly not what teachers unions are about. They are about accumulating the power necessary to advocate for the interests of their members. In a moment of candor, Bob Chanin, former general counsel of the National Education Association, explained the key to the union's effectiveness: "Despite what some among us would like to believe, it is NOT because of our creative ideas. It is NOT because of the merit of our positions. It is NOT because we care about children, and it is NOT because we have a vision of a great public school for every child. NEA and its affiliates are effective advocates because we have power."

The disarming image of teachers unions as Mary Poppins has begun to morph into that of a burly autoworker, as teachers union advocacy has become more militant in recent years. As states attempt to trim very generous benefit packages for

teachers, the unions have organized large demonstrations, oc-
cupied state capitols, and chanted angry slogans. The public
image of teachers unions fighting like autoworkers for the
benefit to retire at 55 with full medical coverage and 66 percent of their peak salary while the economy is in shambles
and the quality of their industry stagnates has done much to
undermine the doting aunt or uncle meme. The angry slogans
emanating from Diane Ravitch's and Valerie Strauss's Twitter
feeds may soothe disgruntled teachers, but they are eroding
the public perception that teachers unions are somehow different from other interest groups. Media and policy elites are
increasingly treating teachers union claims with the same
skepticism that they used to apply only to other interest
groups.

---

*We can look to other public employees, such as members
of the armed forces, who still do not have collective bargaining rights, to see how progress [for teachers] could
have occurred without unionization.*

A third factor is that unions have significant influence
over who is elected or appointed to negotiate with them over
pay, benefits, and work conditions. In the private sector, the
power of unions is constrained by the competing organized
interests of management. When they sit down to negotiate
pay, benefits, and work conditions, members of management
are inclined to represent the interests of shareholders, not
those of employees. But in education, as in other public-sector
collective bargaining, the interests of employees are represented on both sides of the table. The employees, as citizens,
can organize, finance, and vote for elected officials who favor
the union's interests. It is precisely for this reason that public
employees historically did not have collective bargaining rights.

But didn't the lack of collective bargaining rights sometimes leave teachers vulnerable to arbitrary and discriminatory

treatment by school administrators? Yes, but unionization and collective bargaining were neither necessary nor efficient means of correcting those abuses. We can look to other public employees, such as members of the armed forces, who still do not have collective bargaining rights, to see how progress could have occurred without unionization. The military, like public schools, was once racially segregated. African American servicemen and servicewomen were treated horribly. And sometimes officers treated all soldiers in an arbitrary and unfair manner. These abuses were not corrected by unionization and collective bargaining in the military. They were corrected by executive orders and changing legislation governing those public employees. The same path could have been taken with public school employees without the political distortions that public employee unions introduce by virtue of having their interests represented on both sides of the bargaining table.

It may have taken longer than many would like to integrate the military, expand the roles of women in the armed forces, and end "don't ask, don't tell," but we were able to achieve all of those through an open, public process of changing laws and regulations. Unionized collective bargaining might also have addressed those issues, but it would have been done mostly behind closed doors and would have been accompanied by provisions to protect the narrow interests of the unions at the expense of the public interest. Perhaps the use of drones would have been restricted because it displaces jobs for Air Force pilots; perhaps there would be caps on the hours soldiers could engage in combat. Who knows what else a unionized military might have produced? The point is we rightly restrict the ability of members of the armed forces from unionizing and engaging in collective bargaining, just as we once did and could again for teachers. The claim that public employees have a "right" to unionize and collectively bargain and that exercising this "right" necessarily advances the public interest is obviously false.

The proper mechanism for improving compensation and work conditions in the public sector is through changes in law and regulation. The salary, benefits, job security, and work conditions of public employees are just as much a matter of public policy as the work that those employees are supposed to do. We don't allow smoky backroom deals arrived at in collective bargaining to dictate the goals, structure, or existence of the public education system, so neither should we use that process to determine compensation and work condition policies.

What evidence is there that teachers unions have actually had negative effects on students and the education system? The research literature generally finds that unionization is associated with higher per-pupil costs and lower student achievement, but those findings are not very large and are sometimes inconsistent. A 1996 article by Caroline Hoxby in the *Quarterly Journal of Economics* is widely considered the most methodologically rigorous analysis of the issue. Claremont Graduate University professor Charles Kerchner described Hoxby's study in a literature review prepared for the National Education Association as "the most sophisticated of the econometric attempts to isolate a union impact on the student results and school operations . . ." Hoxby finds that unionization is associated with higher student dropout rates as well as higher spending.

But the reality is that it is very hard to produce rigorous research on the effects of teachers unions on education. For one thing, teachers unions are powerful and active almost everywhere. Even in states without collective bargaining, the unions push state legislatures to put into law what is normally put into collective bargaining agreements. This is less than ideal for the unions, because they don't collect dues in exchange for pushing through legislation like they can for representing members to achieve the same ends through collective bargaining. Unions operate these money-losing operations in right-to-work states to make sure that there is no meaningful policy variation on their key issues. They'd rather that we not discover that the world does not end without a mandatory step-and-ladder pay scale, fair dismissal procedures, and favorable work rules. The lack of policy variation hinders researchers, because outcomes are not likely to be very different where the policies are not very different.

But we don't need a wealth of evidence on teachers unions specifically as long as we know about the effects of interest groups and recognize that teachers unions are indeed interest groups. Seeking to produce evidence on the effects of each interest group separately, especially when there are empirical challenges to doing so, is a bit like trying to prove that gravity operates in every room of a house. We could drop a bowling ball in each room to see if it hits the floor, but sometimes there are tables, couches, or beds in the way. If we don't get the result we expected, it doesn't mean that gravity only applies in certain places; it just means that research constraints prevent us from seeing in a particular situation what we know to be true in general.

In general, we know that interest groups advocate for the benefits of their members, even if it comes at the expense of others. We know that teachers unions are interest groups. And we know that the interests of teachers unions are not entirely consistent with the needs of students and taxpayers. Thus, teachers unions are likely to be negative forces for the education system and certainly should not be seen as helpful. The most rigorous research that does exist bears this out, but we also know this from our more general knowledge of how interest groups affect policy.

It is not currently practical to forbid the unionization of teachers, as we forbid the unionization of members of the armed forces. But if we want to limit the ability of teachers unions to advance their own interests at the expense of children, their families, and taxpayers, we need to consider ways of restricting their ability to engage in collective bargaining. Restricting collective bargaining would force teachers unions to pursue their interests through the legislative process, where competing interests might have a better chance to check their power. And forcing unions to operate through legislation rather than backroom collective-bargaining negotiations would improve transparency, which could also place a check on the unions' ability to satisfy their own interests at the expense of others.

. . . we know that the interests of teachers unions are not entirely consistent with the needs of students and taxpayers. Thus, teachers unions are likely to be negative forces for the education system and certainly should not be seen as helpful.

Richard Kahlenberg places his faith in "democratically elected representatives of educators," that is, the teachers unions, to safeguard the interests of children. Note that he does not say the democratically elected representatives of the people, or the voters. Kahlenberg is perfectly comfortable with a school system whose policies and practices are dominated by its employees, not by the citizens who pay for it or by the families whose children are compelled to attend it. Rather than seeing a system controlled by its employees as one characterized by self-interested adults maximizing their benefits at the expense of children, Kahlenberg sees it as the ideal.

In my ideal vision, we would put our faith in parents, not teachers unions, to represent the interests of children. If we had a robust system of parental school choice, I would have no problem with teachers unions and collective bargaining. In the private sector, if unions ask for too much, at least they experience the natural consequences of destroying their own companies or industries (to wit, the auto industry). But in the public sector, unions are almost entirely insulated from the consequences of making unreasonable demands, since governments never go out of business. Public sector unions can drive total revenue for their industry higher without any improvements in productivity simply by getting public officials to increase taxes.

Unfortunately, we lack a robust system of school choice and instead have to rely on democratic institutions, like school boards and state legislatures, to determine most school policies and practices. But unless we also restrict the collective bargaining rights of school employees, teachers unions will dominate the decisions of those democratic institutions, given their advantages in funding and organization, to distort elections and policy decisions.

Teachers unions almost certainly raise salaries and benefits, as Kahlenberg suggests, but that doesn't necessarily attract better teachers if the salary schedule does nothing to reward excellence. Similarly, union-imposed dismissal procedures make it virtually impossible to fire ineffective teachers. The alignment that Kahlenberg sees between teachers unions' desire to increase education spending and the interests of students would only be a real concordance if the unions facilitated the use of those funds in ways that actually improved outcomes.

10

Teachers' Unions Weaken American Education

Lindsey Burke

Lindsey Burke is a policy analyst in the Domestic Policy Studies Department at the Heritage Foundation.

Teachers' unions are at the root of most of the problems with US education. These unions force their members to pay dues, and then use those dues to support liberal political causes that are opposed by most members. Teachers' unions hurt local governments by lobbying for increased unaffordable pensions and benefits for their members. The unions also hurt students by opposing reforms that would allow students to choose which schools they want to attend. The solution to improving education is, therefore, not more grants from the federal government, but a weakening of union power.

The Senate will soon consider creating a $10 billion "Education Jobs Fund." The measure has already been included in a war funding bill passed in early July [2010] by the House. Union influence and power has continued to prevent meaningful education reform, and another public education bailout from Washington will further empower unions, which will make it more difficult for states to implement the common-sense changes that are needed to improve American education in the long run.

Lindsey Burke, "Creating a Crisis: Unions Stifle Education Reform," *Heritage Foundation,* July 20, 2010. Copyright © 2010 by The Heritage Foundation. All rights reserved. Reproduced by permission.

Education Unions Funded by Forced and Voluntary Contributions

Teachers unions generate the bulk of their capital from their millions of dues-paying members. During the 2009–2010 school year, the National Education Association (NEA) national affiliate received $162 per teacher and $93 per public school staff member. Public education employees also contribute an average of $300 per year to their state and local union affiliates.

Today, employees in 28 states can lose their jobs if they refuse to join a union or pay union dues. In most states, teachers unions can use their members' dues to contribute to campaigns and other political causes. In all but five states, even though members elect their union representatives, "union leaders appear to pursue an agenda disconnected from the concerns of their members."

With a budget of more than $355 million, the NEA spends more on campaign contributions than Exxon-Mobil, Microsoft, Wal-Mart, and the AFL-CIO combined.

An NEA member survey found that 50 percent of dues-paying members identified themselves as being more conservative than liberal, but 91 percent of the NEA's campaign and political contributions went to Democrats or left-leaning causes. The two major teachers unions make 95 percent of their political contributions to Democrats.

Teachers unions also dominate election spending. According to the Federal Election Commission, as of July 2010, unions had contributed $9.7 million of the $24.7 million in campaign spending, representing 39 percent of total expenditures. By contrast, corporations had spent just $3.4 million.

With a budget of more than $355 million, the NEA spends more on campaign contributions than ExxonMobil, Microsoft,

Wal-Mart, and the AFL-CIO combined. During the 2007–2008 election cycle, the NEA and American Federation of Teachers (AFT) spent more than $71 million on campaigns for issues and candidates, spending more than $100 per teacher in five states. In addition to the millions in campaign contributions, the NEA provides hundreds of thousands of dollars in member dues to left-leaning groups such as Planned Parenthood, the Service Employees International Union, and Health Care for America Now. The AFT funds groups that include the Rainbow PUSH coalition and ACORN.

National union leaders receive plush salaries. The national affiliate of the NEA paid more than 370 of its employees salaries of $100,000 or more in 2009. Several executive board members earned well over $200,000. NEA President Dennis Van Roekel was provided a salary of slightly under $300,000, and Vice President Lily Eskelsen received over $240,000 in 2009. NEA Treasurer Rebecca Pringle received $321,000 last year.

Unions Weaken American Education

Over the past five decades, unions have successfully lobbied to prevent public education employees from having to contribute to the cost of their own health insurance premiums, for increases in pensions and other benefits, and against provisions such as parental school choice. They have also fought against tenure reform and merit pay for teachers and, more recently, have been at the forefront of the [Barack] Obama Administration's push for another $10 billion public education bailout.

Democratic leadership claims that the creation of a $10 billion Education Jobs Fund would save 140,000 public education jobs. Assuming this figure, each job "saved" would cost more than $70,000; the average teacher salary for the 2008–2009 school year was $54,000. Moreover, according to the U.S. Census Bureau, 57 percent of public school teachers nationally are unionized. Assuming a conservative estimate of $300 per teacher in average union dues to state and local affiliates, teachers unions have around $24 million in dues at stake in the Education Jobs Fund.

In states with school choice provisions for children ...,
teachers unions are typically the primary opponents of
such options.

The $10 billion public education bailout being considered by Congress would be on top of the nearly $100 billion appropriated to the Department of Education through the so-called stimulus bill in 2009. But the Administration seems to be withholding these funds from states with weaker union support. Of note, applications from states with demonstrably improved academic track records were rejected by the Department of Education during the review process for phase I Race to the Top (RTTT) grants, the Obama Administration's signature education reform program. Department reviewers for the RTTT grant initiative noted that certain states did not have enough union "buy-in" for their reform plans. Notably, the two states that won RTTT grants of $500 million and $100 million, respectively—Tennessee and Delaware—had nearly 100 percent union buy-in.

Researchers have found that public school teachers "have more compressed wage structures [that is, there is less of a gap between the highest and lowest paid] than (overwhelmingly nonunion) private schools, even when the private schools nominally have similar pay schedules." Unions also create barriers to entry into the teaching profession by opposing alternative teacher certification programs that would allow more mid-career professionals and those without traditional teaching degrees into the classroom.

In states with school choice provisions for children (such as tax credit and deduction programs, public and private school choice, charter schools, virtual education, and homeschooling), teachers unions are typically the primary opponents of such options. This outcome has been particularly unfortunate in Washington, D.C., where the highly successful and overwhelmingly popular D.C. Opportunity Scholarship Program, which provides vouchers of up to $7,500 for low-income children to attend a private school of their choice, is being phased out primarily because of pressure from teachers unions.

The Failed Status Quo

Another federal bailout for education from Washington would ultimately help unions perpetuate the failed status quo. Instead of seeking more federal assistance, state leaders should consider alternatives to the traditional paradigm that is acceptable to the NEA and AFT, such as reforming public pension plans, requiring teachers to contribute to their health insurance premiums, and reforming hiring practices and teacher compensation.

Many of the problems plaguing American education today can be attributed directly to union power, which can be curtailed through common-sense reforms at the state level. Breaking the stranglehold from these unions is the first step toward making long-term, meaningful education reform.

11

Right-to-Work Laws Free Workers from Coercive Union Control

Jeff Jacoby

Jeff Jacoby is a columnist for the Boston Globe *newspaper.*

In most states, unions force all employees to pay dues, whether they support the union or not. Most Americans are opposed to this. State right-to-work laws give individuals the right to opt out of paying union dues. Union leaders claim that dues are necessary so that members do not get a free ride. However, this is simply a pretext. Unions demand the right to bargain collectively for all workers, and then make the workers pay for the privilege. Unions, which claim to be about democracy and the right to choice, are in fact built on coercion and undemocratic principles.

Soon—perhaps today—Governor Mitch Daniels will sign legislation making Indiana the nation's 23rd right-to-work state. Labor unions angrily oppose the change, but their opposition has no legitimate or principled basis.

Pro-Choice, Not Anti-Union

State right-to-work laws, authorized by the Taft-Hartley Act of 1947, are not anti-union. They are pro-choice: They protect workers from being forced to join or pay fees to a labor union as a condition of keeping a job. In non-right-to-work states, employees who work in a "union shop" are compelled to fork over part of each paycheck to a labor organization—even if they want nothing to do with unions, let alone to be represented by one.

Far from rejecting compulsion, Big Labor now fights tooth and nail to defend it. And no wonder: Unions have long since squandered the affection of the American public.

Laws like the one Indiana is poised to enact simply make union support voluntary. Hoosiers can't be required to kick back part of their wages to the Republican Party or the Methodist Church or the Animal Liberation Front; the new measure will ensure that they don't have to give a cut of everything they earn to labor unions, either.

Most Americans regard compulsory unionism as unconscionable. In a new Rasmussen survey, 74 percent of likely voters say non-union workers should not have to pay dues against their will. Once upon a time, labor movement giants like Samuel Gompers, a founder of the American Federation of Labor, agreed. "I want to urge devotion to the fundamentals of human liberty—the principles of voluntarism," declared Gompers in his last speech to the AFL in 1924. "No lasting gain has ever come from compulsion."

But far from rejecting compulsion, Big Labor now fights tooth and nail to defend it. And no wonder: Unions have long since squandered the affection of the American public. In the years right after World War II, more than one-third of the US workforce was unionized; now the union membership rate is just 11.8 percent, and most of those members are government employees. In the productive economy, Americans continue to flee from organized labor. Last year only 6.9 percent of workers at private companies belonged to unions.

So as a matter of by-any-means-necessary expediency, it is easy to understand why Big Labor long ago embraced what liberal scholar Robert Reich (later Bill Clinton's secretary of labor) dubbed "the necessity for coercion." In order "to maintain themselves," Reich said in 1985, "unions have got to have some ability to strap their members to the mast." Or, as Don Corleone might have put it, to make them an offer they can't refuse.

But is there any ethical reason—any honorable basis—for the union shop?

Union Coercion

Labor and its allies are ruthless, and usually quite effective, in beating down right-to-work bills. Indiana will be the first state in more than a decade that has succeeded in banning labor contracts that oblige all employees to pay money to a union as a condition of employment. (A similar bill in New Hampshire last year was vetoed by Governor John Lynch.) No-holds-barred vehemence in defense of principle might be understandable. But what legitimate principle are the unions defending?

To hear them tell it, they only object to "free riders." Labor leaders claim it would be unjust to allow employees to avoid paying for the unions that negotiate benefits on their behalf. "There's always going to be a certain amount of the population that will take something for free if they can get it for free," says Nancy Guyott, head of the Indiana AFL-CIO.

The labor movement was born in freedom and choice. That's not what it stands for anymore.

That's not a principle, it's a shameless pretext. Unions demand monopoly bargaining power—the right to exclusively represent everyone in a workplace—and then insist that each of those workers must pay for the privilege. This is the "principle" of the squeegee man who aggressively wipes your windshield when you stop at a red light, then demands that you pay for the service he has rendered you.

By the union's "free rider" logic, shouldn't all voters be forced to subscribe to a daily newspaper, since all of them benefit from its journalism? And shouldn't every company be compelled to support the Chamber of Commerce, which lobbies on behalf of business, whether individual firms ask it to or not?

The passion with which Big Labor fights right-to-work helps explain why so many Americans have abandoned unions. The labor movement was born in freedom and choice. That's not what it stands for anymore.

12

Right-to-Work Laws Hurt Workers, Society, and the Economy

David Madland, Karla Walter, and Ross Eisenbrey

David Madland is director of the American Worker Project at the Center for American Progress Action Fund. Karla Walter is a senior policy analyst with the project. Ross Eisenbrey is vice president of the Economic Policy Institute.

Right-to-work laws force unions to provide services to members who do not pay dues, a condition imposed on no other organization. In addition, right-to-work laws do not create jobs; hurt workers by lowering salaries and benefits; make workplaces less safe; and damage the middle-class. Since unions increase democratic participation, right-to-work laws, by weakening unions, will also harm democracy. Advocates of right-to-work laws support them not because they will actually benefit workers or society, but because they are politically committed to crippling the union movement.

In states where the law exists, "right-to-work" makes it illegal for workers and employers to negotiate a contract requiring everyone who benefits from a union contract to pay their fair share of the costs of administering it. Right-to-work has nothing to do with people being forced to be union members.

David Madland, Karla Walter, and Ross Eisenbrey, "Right-To-Work 101," *Center for American Progress*, February 2, 2012. Copyright © 2012 by the Center for American Progress. All rights reserved. Reproduced by permission.

Federal law already guarantees that no one can be forced to be a member of a union, or to pay any amount of dues or fees to a political or social cause they don't support. What right-to-work laws do is allow some workers to receive a free ride, getting the advantages of a union contract—such as higher wages and benefits and protection against arbitrary discipline—without paying any fee associated with negotiating on these matters.

That's because the union must represent all workers with the same due diligence regardless of whether they join the union or pay it dues or other fees and a union contract must cover all workers, again regardless of their membership in or financial support for the union. In states without right-to-work laws, workers covered by a union contract can refuse union membership and pay a fee covering only the costs of workplace bargaining rather than the full cost of dues.

There is scant evidence these laws create jobs, help workers, or are good for a state's economy, as supporters claim. Instead, these laws weaken unions and thereby hurt workers, the middle class, and local economies. We present here a Right-to-Work 101 so that the debate over right-to-work laws proceeds based on the facts.

Right-to-work laws have not increased employment growth in the 22 states that have adopted them.

Right-to-Work Laws Don't Create Jobs

Researchers who study the impact of right-to-work laws find that these laws do not create jobs—despite supporters' claims to the contrary. The Indiana Chamber of Commerce, for example, claims that "unionization increases labor costs," and therefore makes a given location less attractive to capital. The purpose, then, of right-to-work laws is to undermine unions and therefore lower wages in a given state, thus attracting more companies into the state.

But in practice this low-road strategy for job creation just doesn't pan out. Despite boosters' promises of job creation, researchers find that right-to-work had "no significant positive impact whatsoever on employment" in Oklahoma, the only state to have adopted a right-to-work law over the past 25 years—until Indiana did so days ago—and consequently the best example of how a new adopter of right-to-work laws might fare in today's economy. In fact, both the number of companies relocating to Oklahoma and the total number of manufacturing jobs in the state fell by about a third since it adopted such a law in 2001.

Indeed, most right-to-work advocates' purported evidence of job growth is based on outdated research and misleading assertions. An Indiana Chamber of Commerce-commissioned study found right-to-work states had higher employment growth between 1977 and 2008 compared to states without a right-to-work law, but much of that growth could be attributed to other factors. Those factors included the states' infrastructure quality, and even its weather—which the study ignored.

Recent research from the Economic Policy Institute that controlled for these factors finds that right-to-work laws have not increased employment growth in the 22 states that have adopted them.

Right-to-Work Laws Hurt Workers

Right-to-work laws lower worker pay and benefits and make workplaces more dangerous for all workers—whether unionized or not—by weakening unions.

Unions have a significant and positive effect on the wages and benefits of union and nonunion workers alike. Unionized workers are able to bargain for better wages, benefits, and work conditions than they would otherwise receive if negotiating individually. The effect on the average worker—unionized or not—of working in a right-to-work state is to earn approximately $1,500 less per year than a similar worker in a state without such a law.

Right-to-work laws also may hurt workplace safety.

Workers in right-to-work states are also significantly less likely to receive employer-provided health insurance or pensions. If benefits coverage in non-right-to-work states were lowered to the levels of states with these laws, 2 million fewer workers would receive health insurance and 3.8 million fewer workers would receive pensions nationwide.

The fact that unionization raises people's wages and benefits is borne out by surveys of union members and by common sense. Unions also affect the wages and benefits of non-union workers by setting standards that gradually become norms throughout industries. To compete for workers, non-union employers in highly unionized industries have to pay their workers higher wages. And unions support government policies (such as minimum-wage laws) that raise workers' pay.

Right-to-work laws also may hurt workplace safety. For instance, the occupational-fatality rate in the construction industry—one of the most hazardous in terms of workplace deaths—is 34 percent higher in right-to-work states than in states without such laws. And one academic study finds that increasing union density has a positive effect on workplace safety in states with no right-to-work laws (for every 1 percent increase in unionization rates there is a 0.35 percent decline in construction fatality rates), but in right-to-work states, the effect of union density on safety disappears.

Unions are democratic organizations: If employees didn't like their contracts, they would vote to reject the contract, vote to change their union officers, or vote to get rid of their union—all of which can be done under current law.

Right-to-Work Laws Weaken the Middle Class and Hurt Small Business

By weakening unions right-to-work laws also weaken the middle class. From pushing for fair wages and good benefits, to encouraging citizens to vote, to supporting Social Security and advocating for family-leave benefits, unions make the middle class strong by giving workers a voice in both the market and our democracy.

When right-to-work laws lower the wages and benefits of area workers, they also threaten to reduce the number of jobs in the economy by reducing consumer demand.

Nine of the 10 states with the lowest percentage of workers in unions—Mississippi, Arkansas, South Carolina, North Carolina, Georgia, Virginia, Tennessee, Texas, and Oklahoma— are right-to-work states. All of them also are saddled with a relatively weak middle class. The share of total income going to the middle class—defined as the middle 60 percent of the population—in each of these states is below the national average.

If unionization rates increased by 10 percentage points nationwide, the typical middle-class household—unionized or not—would earn $1,479 more each year. In fact, dollar for dollar, strengthening unions is nearly as important to the middle class as boosting college-graduation rates.

Since few small businesses are ever unionized, changing union regulations won't affect them. Yet unlike big manufacturers who can choose which state to expand into, most small businesses are rooted in a local community and dependent on local consumers. When right-to-work laws lower the wages and benefits of area workers, they also threaten to reduce the number of jobs in the economy by reducing consumer demand.

The Economic Policy Institute estimates that for every $1 million in wage cuts, six jobs are lost in the service, retail, construction, real estate, and other local industries. For big manufacturers that sell their products all over the globe, this may be less important.

For small businesses that depend on local sales, reducing the amount of disposable income in local employees' pockets can be devastating.

Right-to-Work Laws Create Rules That Would Hurt All Organizations but Only Apply to Unions

The corporate lobbyists who push for right-to-work legislation—such as the Chamber of Commerce and the National Right to Work Committee—want unions to operate under a set of rules that none of them accept for themselves. These lobbyists would never think of serving the interests of companies that refuse to pay dues to their organizations, yet they want unions to do so in order to drain their resources.

The Chamber of Commerce and National Right to Work Committee want unions to be the only organizations in the country that are required to provide full services to individuals who pay nothing for them.

Federal law already guarantees every worker who is represented by a union equal and nondiscriminatory representation—meaning unions must provide the same services, vigorous advocacy, and contractual rights and benefits. This guarantee applies regardless of whether the employee is a union member. So if a non-dues-paying employee encounters a problem at work, the union is required to provide that individual full representation at no charge.

By contrast, the Chamber of Commerce and other employer organizations restrict some of their most valuable services to dues-paying members. When asked if they would agree to provide all services to any interested business, even if that business does not pay dues, Chamber representatives explained that they could not do that because dues are the primary source of Chamber funding and it would be unfair to other dues-paying members. And that certainly makes sense—for unions as well as the Chamber.

The Chamber of Commerce and National Right to Work Committee want unions to be the only organizations in the country that are required to provide full services to individuals who pay nothing for them. This is no different than enabling some American citizens to opt out of paying taxes while making available all government services. This is not an agenda to increase employee rights but rather to undermine the viability of independent-employee organizations.

Right-to-Work Laws Are Bad for Our Political Democracy

Right-to-work laws infringe on the democratic rights of the electorate by weakening unions. Unions help boost political participation among ordinary citizens and convert this participation into an effective voice for pro-middle-class policies. By weakening unions, they are less able to advocate for pro-worker policies within our government and help get workers out to vote.

Research shows that for every percentage-point increase in union density, voter turnout increased by 0.2 to 0.25 percentage points. This means that if unionization rates were 10 percentage points higher during the 2008 presidential election, 2.6 million to 3.2 million more citizens would have voted.

Unions also help translate workers' interests to elected officials and ensure that government serves the economic needs of the middle class. They do this by encouraging the public to support certain policies as well as by directly advocating for specific reforms. Unions were critical in securing government policies that support the middle class such as Social Security, the Affordable Care Act, family leave, and minimum-wage laws.

Indeed, this may be a large part of why many conservatives support right-to-work laws. Research demonstrates that supporters' claims that these laws will create jobs and strengthen local economies are not credible. Instead, supporters may back these laws as a pretext for attacking an already weakened union movement in hopes of crippling it as a political force and as an advocate for all workers.

The bottom line: Right-to-work laws work against the critical needs of our economy, our society, and our democracy.

Organizations to Contact

The editors have compiled the following list of organizations concerned with the issues debated in this book. The descriptions are derived from materials provided by the organizations. All have publications or information available for interested readers. The list was compiled on the date of publication of the present volume; the information provided here may change. Be aware that many organizations take several weeks or longer to respond to inquiries, so allow as much time as possible.

AFL-CIO (American Federation of Labor and Congress of Industrial Organizations)
815 16th St. NW, Washington, DC   20006
(202) 637-5000
website: www.aflcio.org

The AFL-CIO is the largest federation of unions in the United States. Its mission is to improve the lives of working families by organizing and lobbying for economic and social justice. Its website includes statements, press releases, news updates, and essays and articles about the union movement.

American Federation of Teachers (AFT)
555 New Jersey Ave. NW, Washington, DC   20001
(202) 879-4400
website: www.aft.org

The AFT is an American labor union that represents teachers; paraprofessionals and school-related personnel; local, state and federal employees; higher education faculty and staff; and nurses and other health-care professionals, and is affiliated with the AFL-CIO. The union has more than three thousand local affiliates nationwide and more than 1.3 million members. Its website includes news, reports, and press releases. Its periodical publications include *American Teacher, American Educator, AFT On Campus, PSRP Reporter, Healthwire* and *Public Employee Advocate.*

Cato Institute

1000 Massachusetts Ave. NW, Washington, DC   20001-5403
(202) 842-0200 • fax: (202) 842-3490
website: www.cato.org

The Cato Institute is a libertarian public policy research foundation dedicated to increasing the understanding of public
policies based on the principles of limited government, free
markets, individual liberty, and peace. It publishes the trian-
nual *Cato Journal*, the periodic *Cato Policy Analysis*, and a bi-
monthly newsletter, *Cato Policy Review*. Its website also includes articles such as "Freeing Labor Markets by Reforming
Union Laws" and "Right-to-Work Laws: Libery, Prosperity,
and Quality of Life."

Economic Policy Institute (EPI)

1333 H St. NW, Suite 300, East Tower
Washington, DC   20005-4707
(202) 775-8810 • fax: (202) 775-0819
e-mail: researchdept@epi.org
website: www.epi.org

The Economic Policy Institute (EPI) is a nonprofit Washington think tank that focuses on the economic policy interests
of low- and middle-income workers. It conducts research,
publishes studies and books, briefs policymakers, provides
support to activists, and provides information to the media
and public. Its website includes research reports, news reports,
issue briefs, and more, including articles such as "How Unions
Can Help Restore the Middle Class" and "As Unions Decline,
Inequality Rises."

The Heritage Foundation

214 Massachusetts Ave. NE, Washington, DC   20002-4999
(202) 546-4400 • fax: (202) 546-8328
e-mail: info@heritage.org
website: www.heritage.org

The Heritage Foundation is a research and educational institute that promotes conservative public policies based on the
principles of free enterprise, limited government, individual

freedom, traditional American values, and a strong national defense. Its website includes articles and policy briefs on unions, including articles such as "Why Unions Want Higher Taxes" and "Empower Workers, Not Unions with Political Agendas."

The International Labour Organization (ILO)
4 route des Morillons, Geneva 22   CH-1211
  Switzerland
+41 (0) 22 799 6111 • fax: +41 (0) 22 798 8685
e-mail: ilo@ilo.org
website: www.ilo.org

The International Labour Organization is a United Nations agency that is devoted to advancing opportunities for women and men to obtain decent and productive work in conditions of freedom, equity, security, and human dignity. Its main aims are to promote rights at work, encourage decent employment opportunities, enhance social protection, and strengthen dialogue in handling work-related issues. The ILO publishes numerous publications about global labor, including *Global Employment Trends 2011* and *Towards Decent Work in Sub-Saharan Africa*. Many of these publications are available free from the organization's website.

National Education Association (NEA)
1201 Sixteenth St. NW, Washington, DC   20036
(202) 883-8400 • fax: (202) 822-7974
website: www.nea.org

The NEA is the largest union in the United States, representing public school teachers and other support personnel, faculty, and staffers at colleges and universities, retired educators, and college students preparing to become teachers. Two of NEA's publications are the monthly magazine *NEA Today Online* and the biannual report *Thoughts and Action*.

US Bureau of Labor Statistics
Postal Square Bldg., 2 Massachusetts Ave. NE
Washington, DC   20212-0001

(202) 691-5200
website: www.bls.gov

The Bureau of Labor Statistics is the principal fact-finding agency for the federal government in the field of labor economics and statistics. It publishes a range of publications, including *Monthly Labor Review* (available for pdf download) and *The Editor's Desk*, a daily updated online feature. Its website includes many articles and publications about unions in the United States.

US Department of Labor

200 Constitution Ave. NW, Washington, DC 20210
(866) 487-2365
website: www.dol.gov

The Department of Labor is the United States cabinet department responsible for occupational safety, wage and hour standards, unemployment insurance benefits, reemployment services, and some economic statistics. Its website includes numerous articles and reports on unions in the United States.

World Trade Organization (WTO)

Centre William Rappard, Rue de Lausanne 154
Geneva 21 CH-1211
  Switzerland
+41 (0) 22 739 5111 • fax: +41 (0) 22 731 4206
e-mail: enquiries@wto.org
website: www.wto.org

WTO is an international organization that establishes rules dealing with the trade between nations. Its mission is to provide a forum for negotiating agreements aimed at reducing obstacles to international trade and ensuring a level playing field for all, thus contributing to economic growth and development. WTO publishes trade statistics, research, studies, reports, and the journal *World Trade Review*. Recent publications are available on the WTO website.

Bibliography

Books

Oleg Atbashian — *Shakedown Socialism: Unions, Pitchforks, Collective Greed, the Fallacy of Economic Equality, and Other Optical Illusions of "Redistributive Justice"*. Lebanon, TN: Greenleaf Press, 2009.

Kate Bronfenbrenner — *Global Unions: Challenging Transnational Capital Through Cross-Border Campaigns*. Ithaca, NY: Cornell University Press, 2007.

Joe Burns — *Reviving the Strike: How Working People Can Regain Power and Transform America*. Brooklyn, NY: Ig Publishing, 2011.

Philip Dine — *State of the Unions: How Labor Can Strengthen the Middle Class, Improve Our Economy, and Regain Political Influence*. New York: McGraw Hill, 2008.

Daniel DiSalvo — *Government Unions and the Bankrupting of America*. Jackson, TN: Encounter Books, 2011.

Philip Dray — *There Is Power in a Union: The Epic Story of Labor in America*. New York: Anchor Books, 2010.

John Nichols   *Uprising: How Wisconsin Renewed the
                      Politics of Protest, from Madison to
                      Wall Street.* New York: Nation Books,
                      2012.

Rod Paige   *The War Against Hope: How Teachers'
                      Unions Hurt Children, Hinder
                      Teachers, and Endanger Public
                      Education.* Nashville, TN: Thomas
                      Nelson, 2006.

James A. Piazza   *Going Global: Unions and
                      Globalization in the United States,
                      Sweden, and Germany.* Lanham, MD:
                      Lexington Books, 2002.

Lois Weiner and   *The Global Assault on Teaching,
Mary Compton,   Teachers, and Their Unions: Stories for
eds.   Resistance.* New York: Palgrave
                      Macmillan, 2008.

Periodicals and Internet Sources

Dennis Cauchon   "Poll: Americans Favor Union
                      Bargaining Rights," *USA Today*,
                      February 22, 2011.
                      www.usatoday.com.

Thomas Cooley   "Why Public Sector Unions Will Go
and Lee Ohanian   the Way of Private Sector Unions,"
                      Forbes, February 25, 2011.
                      www.forbes.com.

Monica Davey   "Indiana Governor Signs a Law
                      Creating a 'Right to Work' State,"
                      New York Times, Feburary 1, 2012.
                      www.nytimes.com.

The Economist "Labour Unions: Are Public Sector Unions Different?," February 23, 2011. www.economist.com/blogs.

The Economist "The Public Sector Unions: The Battle Ahead," January 6, 2011. www.economist.com.

Jonah Goldbert "Public Unions Must Go," *Los Angeles Times*, February 22, 2011. http://articles.latimes.com.

Steven Greenhouse "A Watershed Moment for Public-Sector Unions," *New York Times*, February 18, 2011. www.nytimes.com.

Mark Guarino "Indiana 'Right to Work' Law: What It Means for the Pro-Union Rust Belt," *Christian Science Monitor*, February 7, 2012. www.csmonitor.com.

Hendrik Hertzberg "The Fight for Unions in Wisconsin," *The New Yorker*, March 7, 2011. www.newyorker.com.

Frederick M. Hess and Martin R. West "Taking on the Teachers Unions," AEI.org, March 29, 2006.

Kyle James "In Era of Globalization, Unions Look Beyond Their Own Borders," *DW*, January 22, 2007. www.dw.de.

Diane Ravitch "Why Teacher Unions Are Good for Teachers—and the Public," AFT.org, Winter 2006–2007.

Kathleen Sharp — "Women Are Becoming Unions' New Voices," *New York Times*, November 19, 2011. www.nytimes.com.

Gabor Steingart — "A Casualty of Globalization: Death of the Unions," *Spiegel*, October 27, 2006. www.spiegel.de.

Andy Stern interviewed by Kris Maher — "Are Unions Still Relevant? SEIU's Andy Stern Thinks So, but Also Sees Need for Attitude Adjustment," *Pittsburgh Post-Gazette*, March 17, 2012. www.post-gazette.com.

Index

CPSIA information can be obtained
at www.ICGtesting.com
Printed in the USA
FFOW020951150213

9 780737 761528

[9]